OPPOSING
VIEWPOINTS®
SERIES

Net Neutrality

Other Books of Related Interest

Opposing Viewpoints Series

The Fifth Estate: Extreme Viewpoints from Alternative Media
Hacking and Freedom of Information
Online Filter Bubbles

At Issue Series

Cyberwarfare
Domestic Surveillance
Trial by Internet

Current Controversies Series

The Political Elite and Special Interests
Privacy and Security in the Digital Age
States' Rights and the Role of the Federal Government

> "Congress shall make no law ... abridging the freedom of speech, or of the press."
>
> *First Amendment to the US Constitution*

The basic foundation of our democracy is the First Amendment guarantee of freedom of expression. The Opposing Viewpoints series is dedicated to the concept of this basic freedom and the idea that it is more important to practice it than to enshrine it.

—

OPPOSING
VIEWPOINTS®
SERIES

| Net Neutrality

Kathryn Roberts, Book Editor

GREENHAVEN
PUBLISHING

Published in 2019 by Greenhaven Publishing, LLC
353 3rd Avenue, Suite 255, New York, NY 10010

Cover image: Antonio Guillem/Shutterstock.com

Library of Congress Cataloging-in-Publication Data

Names: Roberts, Kathryn, 1990– editor.
Title: Net neutrality / Kathryn Roberts, book editor.
Description: New York : Greenhaven Publishing, 2019. | Series: Opposing
  viewpoints | Includes bibliographical references and index. | Audience: Grades 9–12.
Identifiers: LCCN 2018001424| ISBN 9781534502970 (library bound) | ISBN
  9781534502987 (pbk.)
Subjects: LCSH: Network neutrality—Juvenile literature. | Internet
  governance—Juvenile literature. | Telecommunication policy—Juvenile
  literature.
Classification: LCC HE7645 .N464 2019 | DDC 384.3/3—dc23
LC record available at https://lccn.loc.gov/2018001424

Manufactured in the United States of America

Website: http://greenhavenpublishing.com

Contents

The Importance of Opposing Viewpoints

Perhaps every generation experiences a period in time in which the populace seems especially polarized, starkly divided on the important issues of the day and gravitating toward the far ends of the political spectrum and away from a consensus-facilitating middle ground. The world that today's students are growing up in and that they will soon enter into as active and engaged citizens is deeply fragmented in just this way. Issues relating to terrorism, immigration, women's rights, minority rights, race relations, health care, taxation, wealth and poverty, the environment, policing, military intervention, the proper role of government—in some ways, perennial issues that are freshly and uniquely urgent and vital with each new generation—are currently roiling the world.

If we are to foster a knowledgeable, responsible, active, and engaged citizenry among today's youth, we must provide them with the intellectual, interpretive, and critical-thinking tools and experience necessary to make sense of the world around them and of the all-important debates and arguments that inform it. After all, the outcome of these debates will in large measure determine the future course, prospects, and outcomes of the world and its peoples, particularly its youth. If they are to become successful members of society and productive and informed citizens, students need to learn how to evaluate the strengths and weaknesses of someone else's arguments, how to sift fact from opinion and fallacy, and how to test the relative merits and validity of their own opinions against the known facts and the best possible available information. The landmark series Opposing Viewpoints has been providing students with just such critical-thinking skills and exposure to the debates surrounding society's most urgent contemporary issues for many years, and it continues to serve this essential role with undiminished commitment, care, and rigor.

The key to the series's success in achieving its goal of sharpening students' critical-thinking and analytic skills resides in its title—

Opposing Viewpoints. In every intriguing, compelling, and engaging volume of this series, readers are presented with the widest possible spectrum of distinct viewpoints, expert opinions, and informed argumentation and commentary, supplied by some of today's leading academics, thinkers, analysts, politicians, policy makers, economists, activists, change agents, and advocates. Every opinion and argument anthologized here is presented objectively and accorded respect. There is no editorializing in any introductory text or in the arrangement and order of the pieces. No piece is included as a "straw man," an easy ideological target for cheap point-scoring. As wide and inclusive a range of viewpoints as possible is offered, with no privileging of one particular political ideology or cultural perspective over another. It is left to each individual reader to evaluate the relative merits of each argument— as he or she sees it, and with the use of ever-growing critical-thinking skills—and grapple with his or her own assumptions, beliefs, and perspectives to determine how convincing or successful any given argument is and how the reader's own stance on the issue may be modified or altered in response to it.

This process is facilitated and supported by volume, chapter, and selection introductions that provide readers with the essential context they need to begin engaging with the spotlighted issues, with the debates surrounding them, and with their own perhaps shifting or nascent opinions on them. In addition, guided reading and discussion questions encourage readers to determine the authors' point of view and purpose, interrogate and analyze the various arguments and their rhetoric and structure, evaluate the arguments' strengths and weaknesses, test their claims against available facts and evidence, judge the validity of the reasoning, and bring into clearer, sharper focus the reader's own beliefs and conclusions and how they may differ from or align with those in the collection or those of their classmates.

Research has shown that reading comprehension skills improve dramatically when students are provided with compelling, intriguing, and relevant "discussable" texts. The subject matter of these collections could not be more compelling, intriguing, or urgently relevant to today's students and the world they are poised to inherit. The anthologized articles and the reading and discussion questions that are included with them also provide the basis for stimulating, lively, and passionate classroom debates. Students who are compelled to anticipate objections to their own argument and identify the flaws in those of an opponent read more carefully, think more critically, and steep themselves in relevant context, facts, and information more thoroughly. In short, using discussable text of the kind provided by every single volume in the Opposing Viewpoints series encourages close reading, facilitates reading comprehension, fosters research, strengthens critical thinking, and greatly enlivens and energizes classroom discussion and participation. The entire learning process is deepened, extended, and strengthened.

For all of these reasons, Opposing Viewpoints continues to be exactly the right resource at exactly the right time—when we most need to provide readers with the critical-thinking tools and skills that will serve them well not only in school but also in their careers and their daily lives as decision-making family members, community members, and citizens. This series encourages respectful engagement with and analysis of opposing viewpoints and fosters a resulting increase in the strength and rigor of one's own opinions and stances. As such, it helps make readers "future ready," and that readiness will pay rich dividends for the readers themselves, for the citizenry, for our society, and for the world at large.

Introduction

Since consumer reliance on digital products and the internet has exploded in the past two decades, one of the most hotly debated topics has been the concept of net neutrality.

The principles behind net neutrality lie in preserving consumers' rights to communicate freely online. Net neutrality, in essence, both enables and protects free speech online. It means that internet service providers (ISPs) can't block or discriminate against applications or content, like hampering people's abilities to access websites like Twitter or Facebook or shutting down the availability of someone streaming a speech about their dissatisfaction with the current government. Similar to the way a phone company cannot charge you more for calling a phone with a different area code from yours, net neutrality means that the ISPs cannot dictate what you view or post online.

While the history of the internet finds its beginnings in the 1960s, and the internet as we know and use today exploded in the early 1990s, the term "net neutrality" was not coined until 2003, by Columbia University professor Tim Wu. He created it as an extension of the concept of a common carrier, which has long since been used to describe the role of traditional landline telephone services. According to Wu, the best way to explain net neutrality is that a public information network will end up being most useful if all content, websites, and platforms are treated equally.

But the battle for net neutrality is not without its difficulties and recently has been heavily politicized in the United States, with Democrats generally in favor and Republicans generally against. For many years, ISPs large and small have been accused of violating net neutrality principles, including Comcast, Madison River Communications, and AT&T. As recently as 2017, Verizon was accused of throttling visitors who accessed video-streaming websites like Netflix and YouTube.

In 2015, following the policies of the Obama administration, the Democratic-led Federal Communications Commission (FCC) ruled in favor of net neutrality by taking those principles and classifying broadband access as a telecommunications service, which would give the internet the same protections under Title II of the Communication Act of 1934. In June 2016, the Court of Appeals for the District of Columbia upheld these rules and the FCC's distinction that broadband access is a public utility, like power or landline phones or water, rather than a luxury, like owning a car or traveling on an airplane.

In January 2017, the Trump administration began. President Donald Trump appointed Ajit Pai as the FCC commissioner, which turned the political leanings of the FCC 3–2 in favor of the Republican Party. Pai announced in April that the FCC was considering the reclassification as negatively impacting both the future infrastructure of the internet and the financial viability of smaller ISPs that service the markets that Verizon, AT&T, Comcast, and Time Warner do not. On December 14, 2017, the FCC voted along party lines to repeal the net neutrality rules that classified the principles under Title II of the Communications Act. That day, attorneys general for the states of Washington and New York spearheaded the announcement that they intended to sue the FCC over its decision.

Opposing Viewpoints: Net Neutrality examines both sides of the highly politicized debate over which entity should govern the internet in the United States and additionally offers a window into the potential future of the internet should the net neutrality principles be either maintained or repealed. Through chapters titled "Is Internet Service a Basic Need?," "Should the Internet Be Regulated by the Government?," "Will the Internet Become Segregated Without Net Neutrality?," and "Is It Necessary to Have a Free and Open Internet in the United States?," a diverse array of perspectives attempt to provide a clear understanding for an incredibly complicated, often nebulous topic that is now discussed almost daily on the internet.

CHAPTER 1

Is Internet Service a Basic Need?

Chapter Preface

I t's easy to believe that a vast majority of Americans use the internet every minute of every day. But is it truly something we could live without? Most people will say it's not possible to go without the internet. Without the internet, we cannot get driving directions, cannot connect immediately with friends or family living on the other side of the world, cannot look up recipes to make dinner, cannot watch our favorite shows and movies, cannot order new books or movies or music, and more. This chapter, which features a viewpoint from a college student living in the United States—presumably a so-called digital native—considers the damage a nonneutral internet would bring not just to her ability to browse the internet but to the abilities of other people her age, who may not be able to afford access to an internet that is tiered and turned into a luxury product by the telecommunications companies that are eager to charge more and more for their services.

In Canada, many citizens struggle to afford internet access, with some users giving up other basic needs like food and lodging just so that they may continue to be connected to what they feel is a necessity. And for those Canadians who say they do not have access, a majority say that they do not because of the massive barrier of cost. If cost considerations can impact low-income-earning households, how are such households to take advantage of the vast resources of the internet? And thus, how are they able to express their First Amendment rights, or even learn about the First Amendment, without affordable access to the internet? Continuing on the political considerations of net neutrality, this chapter features the politicized views of whether it is necessary to preserve open internet access for its users, whether they are low-income earners or not.

> "*The Internet is how we communicate and how we work, learn new things, and find out where to go and how to get there.*"

Why Net Neutrality Matters

April Glaser

In the following viewpoint, April Glaser argues that net neutrality is what protects our essential access to the internet, without threat of data throttling or censorship. Good net neutrality rules, the viewpoint asserts, protect websites from unfair policing by ISPs, which at times have limited access or made access difficult to websites that they deem are used for improper acts like copyright infringement—and these company decisions sometimes go on unpoliced for years. Additionally, without the guarantee that all data on the internet is treated equally, ISPs could have the ability to block certain information, including legal and government information. Glaser is a journalist who covers robots, drones, and artificial intelligence for Recode. She previously worked for the Electronic Frontier Foundation (EFF) on the 2014 net neutrality campaign.

As you read, consider the following questions:

1. According to the viewpoint, what is net neutrality?
2. What are the ways in which keeping a free and open internet impacts free speech?
3. Per the viewpoint, why do some internet users prefer to use encrypted browsing, and how will the removal of net neutrality protections negatively impact that?

Right now the FCC is considering a set of rules that would allow Internet providers to offer faster access to some websites that can afford to pay. We need to stop them.

Let's start with the obvious: The Internet is how we communicate and how we work, learn new things, and find out where to go and how to get there. It keeps us connected to those we love and informed of political events that affect our everyday lives.

At EFF, we have fought for almost 25 years to protect a free and open Internet. We depend on the Internet for everything we do, from our efforts to reform broken copyright laws, to our ongoing battles to end the NSA's illegal mass surveillance. More fundamentally, we know that the open Internet makes possible not just our activism, but the work of many others around the world.

That's why we're fighting tooth and nail to defend a concept known as net neutrality. Net neutrality means that Internet providers should treat all data that travels over their networks equally, rather than slowing down or even blocking access to sites of their choosing.

Good net neutrality rules would forbid Internet providers from discriminating against sites that cannot afford to pay a toll for preferential treatment, or sites that are critical of Internet providers or undermine their business models.

That threat is real. In 2005, for example, Canadian ISP Telus blocked access to a website that was used to plan actions by the Telecommunications Workers Union during a strike. And in 2007, AT&T deleted Eddy Vedder's criticism of George W. Bush during a webcasted Pearl Jam concert. Although AT&T was technically acting in the capacity of a content provider, content providers and Internet providers have merged dramatically in the past few years, resulting in the lines becoming uncomfortably blurred. This sort of censorship threatens both innovation and free speech.

Fighting for the Users

Right now the entire architecture of the Internet is under threat. The FCC is about to make a decision that will determine whether or not Internet providers will be allowed to offer faster access to some websites, while leaving others in the slow-lane.

We're calling on the FCC to do the right thing and not allow for rampant discrimination online. Specifically, we're telling the FCC that the Internet needs to be treated as part of our essential communications infrastructure, and that means regulating it as such to protect net neutrality.

Net neutrality is central to all of our efforts to protect and defend digital rights. Let's go through a handful of EFF's issues to explain how.

The Risk to Privacy Conscious Services

Without net neutrality, Internet providers may interfere with access to privacy protecting services and websites or encrypted traffic. We have the right to encrypt our communications because privacy is a human right and it's protected in the US Constitution. Yet, in the past we saw Comcast blocking encrypted traffic to BitTorrent. And in Canada, the broadband provider Rogers Hi-Speed Internet blocked and throttled all encrypted file transfers over their network for five years.

Use of encrypted browsing prevents Internet providers from injecting ads into the pages you view and prevents them from logging your activities to sell to marketers, so they have an economic incentive to keep it easy to spy on you. Without net neutrality, there's no telling what privacy-enabling tools will become unusable at the whim of Internet providers.

The Basic Right of Internet

People may joke that others spend too much time on the internet, but this intricate series of tubes has become an important part of everyday life—so much so that it's become a human rights violation to take it away.

That's according to the United Nations Human Rights Council, which passed a non-binding resolution in June that condemns countries that intentionally take away or disrupt its citizens' internet access.

The resolution was passed last Friday, but was opposed by countries including Russia, China, Saudi Arabia, South Africa, and India. The issue was with the passage that "condemns unequivocally measures to intentionally prevent or disrupt access to our dissemination of information online." More than 70 states supported the resolutions, according to a statement released by Article 19, a British organization that works to promote freedom of expression and information. Thomas Hughes, the executive director of Article 19, wrote:

We are disappointed that democracies like South Africa, Indonesia, and India voted in favour of these hostile amendments to weaken protections for freedom of expression online ... A human rights based approach to providing and expanding Internet access, based on states' existing international human rights obligations, is essential to achieving the Agenda 2030 for Sustainable Development, and no state should be seeking to slow this down.

The resolution notes what many of us already know: It's important to increase access to the internet, as it "facilitates vast opportunities for affordable and inclusive education globally," or provides other resources for education, especially across the digital divide. In accordance with the 2030 Agenda for Sustainable Development, the organization also recognized that the spread of technology has the "great potential to accelerate human progress."

It's all here: your news organizations, your job-hunting resources, and your credit card statements. It's become impossible to live without basic internet access.

Other countries have already stressed the importance of open access, including President Barack Obama, who in 2015 said that "today, high speed broadband is not a luxury, it's a necessity."

The resolution also highlights a number of issues that need to be addressed, including the issue of freedom of expression on the internet. The UN can't enforce resolutions legally. Rather, they're issued to provide guidelines for participating nations and to put pressure on any that may have dissenting views.

"Internet Access Is Now a Basic Human Right," by Carli Velocci, Gizmodo Media Group, July 4, 2016.

An increasing trend in privacy-conscious products is the move to technologies where sensitive data is self hosted, hosted by friends, or resides on an anonymous decentralized network instead of on the servers of a company that law enforcement can easily compel to turn over your data without telling you first.

But many ISPs have rules against people running "servers" at home, prohibiting people from making use of the upstream bandwidth they've paid for. If all bits were treated equally, then it wouldn't matter whether the traffic originated with a server. In other words, if users pay for their bandwidth, then they should be able to use it however they want.

Without good net neutrality protections, we fear that privacy conscious services will be significantly affected, not only because small companies and free software communities most likely won't be able to afford fast-lane access, but also because Internet providers may degrade such services for their own business reasons.

Copyright Policing from Internet Providers

Copyright is routinely cited as an excuse for corporate and government censorship of the Internet. When Comcast blocked all encrypted traffic to BitTorrent back in 2007, they claimed it was because BitTorrent was used for copyright infringement—never mind the many non-infringing uses that were also blocked. Good net neutrality rules would prevent that kind of policing from ISPs, as well as unilateral decisions by ISPs to degrade or block access to sites they allege are infringing or promote infringement.

This is a particular concern as more Internet providers expand into content production and distribution. Network discrimination could be used to herd users towards services the ISPs offer, like Verizon's RedBox, rather than their competitors. Again, good net neutrality rules would not allow Internet providers to direct users to one site over another by speeding up or slowing down online traffic.

Copyright has caused problems for net neutrality before. We've seen bad net neutrality rules with giant holes carved out for ISPs to discriminate based on copyright infringement, such as the 2010 Open Internet order. Carve-outs for copyright are antithetical to the principles of net neutrality, and we're calling on the FCC to create application agnostic, bright line anti-discrimination rules.

Access to Information

Transparency can be a powerful tool. One of our core visions for a more transparent political environment is for government data, court documents and interpretations of the law to be readily accessible online. Access to the law shouldn't be slower than, say, viewing an entertainment website. But without strong net neutrality rules, Internet providers are likely to offer faster access to some websites while impeding our access to information.

The Future of Our Internet

The open Internet is central to projects of social justice and political change. Our democracy cannot afford network discrimination. Money and the whims of Internet providers shouldn't determine who is able to speak to whom and at what rate.

Join us as we call on the FCC to do the right thing: treat all traffic that travels over the Internet equally. The Internet is our future. It's how we communicate, innovate, and organize to better our world. It's our Internet, and we're going to fight to protect it.

> "A less neutral internet leaves too much power to companies who might be inclined to charge more for faster access."

It's an Issue of Class

Chinelo Nkechi Ikem

In the following viewpoint, Chinelo Nkechi Ikem, a college student who presumably grew up as a digital-era native, describes the importance of the internet, arguing that its purpose extends far beyond simple entertainment. While agreeing that a repeal of net neutrality regulations does not mean that ISPs would immediately begin charging extra and prioritizing internet access, Ikem also describes the negative impact those actions would have on her—and others'—ability to keep up-to-date on the news. It would also negatively impact their own ability to share their life with other readers online. Additionally, she describes the differences in political opinion on the importance of net neutrality and touches on how this has become such a partisan issue in recent years. Ikem is a political science and philosophy double major at the University of California, Santa Barbara.

As you read, consider the following questions:

1. The Obama-era net neutrality regulations were put in place to prohibit which actions that could be taken by ISPs?
2. The author claims that rolling back net neutrality regulations would have the strongest negative impact on which social group?
3. Which group most vocally opposed President Barack Obama's stance on internet access protections?

Today, tech companies and websites like Twitter and Netflix are joining forces with politicians and other organizations to protest in favor of net neutrality in a "Day of Action." This is in response to movements by the Federal Communications Commission to revoke regulations that promote net neutrality by essentially allowing internet service providers, or ISPs, the ability to block or alter the speed of certain internet content.

How did we get here? And why is it important?

In statement released on Nov. 10, 2014, Barack Obama said that he would ask the FCC to institute regulations preventing blocking, paid prioritization, and throttling, the slowing down or speeding up of content based on your service provider. The statement also called for full transparency from the FCC, to make sure other points of connection would not be experiencing prioritization either.

In a video, Obama argued that internet service should be treated as a free and open space, recommending that the FCC reclassify internet service as common carriers under Title II of the Communications Act of 1934. That stance was met with opposition from Republicans and major ISPs. That same day the statement was released, Ted Cruz would take to Twitter to call net neutrality "Obamacare for the internet." When asked about his thoughts on net neutrality, Comcast CEO Brian Roberts suggested more government regulation was unnecessary, saying "the idea that we're not going to have an open internet is just not realistic."

Under former FCC chairman Tom Wheeler, on Feb. 26, 2015, in a 3–2 vote, the FCC followed Obama's recommendations and adopted regulations to promote net neutrality. The US Court of Appeals for the DC Circuit upheld the net neutrality regulations against a petition filed by AT&T and several other internet service companies.

Trump-appointed FCC Chairman Ajit Pai is now considering reversing Obama-era net neutrality regulations. On its website, the FCC states that it wants to "rollback heavy-handed internet regulation strives." This means rolling back Obama's prohibitions on paid prioritizing and blocking, allowing internet providers to choose which content gets more speed.

Tech companies are making public moves to prevent these rollbacks. On Netflix, a message appears at the top directing users to a website to learn more about why net neutrality is being threatened. On Twitter, a promoted hashtag #netneutrality is being used by members to share their positions on the issue.

The issue of net neutrality is an important one for many reasons. But first and foremost, it is an issue of class. A less neutral internet leaves too much power to companies who might be inclined to charge more for faster access. And those who can't pay up for fast internet access may be discouraged from creating and accessing content.

Twitter and Netflix can afford to pay more to keep their websites fast and accessible. Smaller companies and individual people can't.

The internet is already not free. Unless you walk to your local library everyday to use a computer, you already pay for use of the internet. Making more internet plans and changing the speeds of certain content only adds more barriers to making the internet a more open and accessible place to share ideas. This unfairly discriminates against poorer communities who can't necessarily pay more for faster internet access. It's one thing to ask that people pay for access to certain television networks packages or phone plans (though we might have to consider those industries more carefully, too). It's an entirely different thing that people pay additional to timely access or provide ideas, services, and content on the internet. The internet has become too integral to the sharing of ideas, to our survival.

As a college student, I am tied to the internet. Not just for my entertainment, but for my homework, for my online subscription to several news sites, and for keeping up to date on progressive movements and actions. If I had to pay more for faster access to certain websites, I don't think I could. If I had to pay more for a blog I ran to be accessible in a timely manner to readers, I couldn't. And that would severely limit the way I interacted with the internet.

One doesn't have to be like me to appreciate why the need for net neutrality is important. If you believe that you should have the freedom to access the internet in the same way as pretty much anyone else in any socio-economic class does, then you believe in net neutrality.

The ACLU recognizes the impact this possible rollback will have on class. The ACLU has a petition that people can sign to stand up for net neutrality. A statement preceding the petition writes "Any proposal that undermines net neutrality violates our freedoms of speech, expression, and inquiry and risks unfair discrimination against low-income communities and communities of color."

There is no guarantee that the removal of these regulations would result in blocking, paid prioritization, or throttling. However, these net neutrality rules need to stay in place to make sure these practices never become a part of how internet access is distributed.

> *"In a 2015 address to the United Nations, Facebook CEO Mark Zuckerberg called internet access 'a basic human right, like access to health care or water.'"*

High-Speed Internet Access Is a Human Right

Sheena Goodyear

In the following viewpoint, Sheena Goodyear argues that many Canadian citizens face serious obstacles when trying to access the internet. She cites a survey of more than one thousand Canadians in which 91 percent of respondents stated that they do have internet access at home, while 30 percent of those who did not claimed cost was their greatest barrier. Goodyear also explains that since 2011, the United Nations has called on all governments to make internet accessible for the entirety of the population, though many organizations claim it is an extremely costly endeavor to do so, and others claim that people do live full lives without internet access. Goodyear is a reporter and senior writer for CBC News.

As you read, consider the following questions:

1. According to the viewpoint, what percentage of people surveyed in Canada have prioritized paying their internet bills over other necessities?
2. Is FCC commissioner Michael O'Rielly's claim that internet access does not meet the threshold to be considered a basic human right realistic?
3. What is the difference between a "basic human right" and "universal service"?

I n an era when some Canadians are cutting back on groceries and skimping on the rent just to stay online, there's a growing argument that high-speed home internet access is no longer a luxury, but a necessity. And the CRTC will soon have to decide whether it agrees.

Internet access has become necessary for employment, education and civic engagement, advocates say. People need to go online to find work, do homework, obtain many government services and stay connected, especially as more programs move toward cloud-based subscription models.

But not everyone has equal access. And that digital divide, advocates say, serves to keep the poorest Canadians from getting a leg up.

A Human Right

The Affordable Access Coalition, made up of public policy, consumer advocate and anti-poverty organizations, is petitioning the CRTC to subsidize internet access for low-income and rural Canadians.

The CRTC will consider the proposal, among others, at public hearings into telecommunications services in April.

Coalition member ACORN Canada, a national organization of low- and moderate-income families, is calling on the CRTC to mandate that $10 per month high-speed internet packages be made available to families and individuals living below Statistics Canada's low-income measure.

"It's no longer a commodity; it's a necessity," ACORN spokeswoman Alejandra Ruiz Vargas told CBC News.

She is not alone in that assertion.

In speech last year, US President Barack Obama proclaimed: "Today, high-speed broadband is not a luxury, it's a necessity."

In a 2015 address to the United Nations, Facebook CEO Mark Zuckerberg called internet access "a basic human right, like access to health care or water."

Facebook, as well as Google, have been investing in expanded internet access in the developing world. Google, meanwhile, announced last week it will provide free ultra-high-speed internet to public housing residents in cities on its Google Fiber network.

Even back in 2011, UN's special rapporteur on freedom of expression called on all governments "to develop a concrete and effective plan of action to make the internet widely available, accessible and affordable to all segments of the population."

But not everyone is sold.

Commissioner Michael O'Rielly of the US Federal Communications Commission said in a speech last year that internet access "doesn't even come close to the threshold to be considered a basic human right."

"People do a disservice by overstating its relevancy or stature in people's lives," he said. "People can and do live without internet access, and many lead very successful lives."

But some Canadians are so desperate to stay online, they forgo other basic needs to do so, says ACORN.

The group recently surveyed 400 of its members and discovered 59 per cent have cut into other budgets to pay their internet bills. Of those, 71 per cent went without food, 64 per cent cut back on recreation and 13 per cent delayed paying their rent.

Eight per cent of those surveyed don't have the internet at home or have cancelled it due to high costs.

"The results were shocking," Vargas said. "Sometimes, we take things for granted."

Universal Service

John Lawford of the Public Interest Advocacy Centre stops short of calling broadband access a human right, but said it should be considered a "universal service," with public policy geared toward making it as widely accessible as possible.

The advocacy centre, also a member of the coalition, suggests that higher-earning Canadians pay a little extra on their own internet bills—about a dollar a month—to subsidize access for those who can't afford it.

That money would fund internet infrastructure in rural areas and subsidies of $10.50 to $20.50 per month for low-income Canadians in urban centres.

But it wouldn't cover the $10-per-month packages ACORN is lobbying for.

"My understanding is that ACORN is going to have to seek further support from say, government, if they really want to get it down to $10," Lawford said.

Keeping Pace

If the CRTC agrees to pursue universal access to broadband internet, it will have to decide what basic service looks like.

Lawford worries that if the benchmark is set too low, Canadians will still be left behind as fibre optic networks expand and raise the bar for what constitutes an acceptable internet.

"As the rest of the networks get upgraded, if there isn't a very careful upgrading of the lowest package for people, this divide in substance will happen again, even though they have quote-unquote internet access, because you won't be able to do anything," he said.

The Public Interest Advocacy Centre suggests a flexible target, based on average download speeds enjoyed by 80 per cent of connected Canadians.

Cost Not the Biggest Barrier: Rogers

The big telecoms will also have their say at the CRTC hearings, where Rogers plans to argue that cost is not the biggest barrier to internet access.

Spokeswoman Jennifer Kett cited a December 2015 Ipsos Reid survey of 1,250 Canadians that found 91 per cent have the internet at home. Among those who don't, 30 per cent cited cost as a barrier, while the other 70 per cent cited a lack of interest or ability.

"So the real challenge is making sure Canadians are getting the most out of their access. That means tackling all barriers such as confidence in security and privacy and increasing digital literacy," Kett said.

> "Vice-President-elect Pence co-sponsored a 2011 bill that would have stripped the FCC of authority to govern Internet access services, as it did in the Open Internet Order."

The Internet Is Not a Public Utility According to the Trump Administration

Kerry Sheehan

In the following viewpoint, written prior to President Donald Trump's inauguration, Kerry Sheehan argues that Trump's team had no intention of protecting net neutrality. The author contends that public opinion tends to be in favor of internet protections, with stringent public opposition to many Republican attempts to limit both net neutrality and the FCC, including the Stop Online Piracy Act (SOPA). The author goes on to describe claims that net neutrality allows consumers to take advantage of valuable services for free and also claims that there is no reason to regulate the internet, because ISPs have not attempted to do so thus far. Sheehan is a lawyer who has worked as a consulting policy strategist with EFF, focusing on intellectual property and net neutrality.

"Trump and His Advisors on Net Neutrality," by Kerry Sheehan, Electronic Frontier Foundation, December 19, 2017. https://www.eff.org/deeplinks/2016/12/trump-and-his-advisers-net-neutrality. Licensed under CC BY 3.0 US.

As you read, consider the following questions:

1. Per the viewpoint, what are examples of bills that attempted to limit net neutrality and the power of the FCC?
2. What are the reasons why Jeffrey Eisenach thinks net neutrality regulations are using the power of the government to obtain free services?
3. Why do Republicans think it is unnecessary for the government to regulate the internet?

Through the combined efforts of EFF and a coalition of public interest groups—and four million of you who wrote in to the FCC—we won carefully tailored and essential net neutrality protections in 2015 and defended them in court in 2016. But how will the incoming Trump administration impact net neutrality in 2017? We've collected a range of statements on the positions of Trump, his transition team, and those who are likely to guide the new administration on this issue.

Trump took a swipe at net neutrality in a November 2014 tweet, stating, "Obama's Attack on the Internet is another top down power grab. Net neutrality is the Fairness Doctrine. Will target Conservative Media."

The Republican Party platform was also critical of net neutrality, and Trump's transition team is stocked with staunch opponents to net neutrality.

Several key members of Trump's transition team belong to a block of Republicans in Congress that have long sought to undermine net neutrality. Vice-President-elect Pence, the chair of Trump's transition team, co-sponsored a 2011 bill that would have stripped the FCC of authority to govern Internet access services, as it did in the Open Internet Order. That bill, the Internet Freedom Act, was sponsored by Rep. Marsha Blackburn, and co-sponsored by Rep. Cathy McMorris Rodgers, Rep. Tom Reed, and Rep. Cynthia Lummis, all vice-chairs on Trump's transition team. Pence (along with vice-chair Rep. Marsha Blackburn, and other members of the transition team) also voted against net neutrality as early as 2006.

Vice-chair Rep. Marsha Blackburn has routinely introduced bills that attempt to block effective net neutrality from every angle. In 2011, she sponsored the Internet Freedom Act, discussed above. She re-introduced it in 2014—this time, the bill would have prohibited the FCC's proposed net neutrality rules from coming into effect and kept the agency from re-issuing such rules in the future, unless explicitly authorized by Congress. That bill was re-introduced again in 2015, this time seeking to nullify the FCC's Open Internet Order and prevent the agency from re-issuing them, unless authorized by Congress. In 2016, Rep. Blackburn sponsored an amendment to the annual budget authorization that would prohibit the use of federal funds to implement any of the FCC's proposed broadband privacy rules. Rep. Blackburn also co-sponsored bills aimed at altering the process through which the FCC can pass rules like the Open Internet Order, and further limiting the FCC's ability to do so.

Rep. Blackburn also co-sponsored two resolutions, one in 2010 and one in 2011 (both with Rep. Cathy McMorris Rodgers, vice-chair) challenging the FCC's authority to implement an earlier version of net neutrality. The 2011 resolution was also co-sponsored by Rep. Nunes another vice-chair, and VP-elect Pence, and passed the US House of Representatives, but died in the Senate. This year, Rep. Blackburn co-sponsored H.R. 2666, the No Rate Regulation of Broadband Internet Access Act, a bill with the potential to undermine net neutrality.

Rep. Blackburn has been highly critical of net neutrality in her public statements. In 2016, in support of a Senate bill attacking net neutrality, Blackburn stated, "[w]e must stop the FCC's Net Neutrality rules, which are nothing more than a Trojan horse for government takeover of the Internet. These overreaching rules will stifle innovation, restrict freedoms, and lead to billions of dollars in new fees and taxes for American consumers." And in 2014, Rep. Blackburn issued a statement insisting that Congress, not the

FCC, should decide when to "regulate the Internet," and called the proposal a "net loser that need[s] to be retired once and for all." Rep. Blackburn responded similarly to the much more limited 2010 Open Internet rules, stating "[t]he FCC is building an Iron Curtain that will restrict more of our freedom." This followed her earlier comment that the FCC had taken a "vampiric leap from its traditional jurisdiction."

Rep. Blackburn hasn't limited her assault on the open Internet to net neutrality: she was also an initial co-sponsor for the Stop Online Piracy Act (SOPA), a disastrous bill that would have allowed for blocking of "blacklisted" websites. Fortunately, the public rose up to protect the Internet back then, too.

Several members of the transition team's executive committee also oppose net neutrality. Rep. Tom Marino disagreed with the commission's Open Internet rules and called the decision a "slippery slope which ultimately endangers our liberty ... regulating the internet is just another way this Administration uses the bureaucracy to allow and condone more regulation and government control." Rep. Chris Collins also opposed the decision, saying "[t]he FCC's actions threaten the innovative culture that makes the Internet one of the world's greatest technologies." He called the decision "a direct threat to Internet freedom" and a "foreshadowing of the big government overregulation that will stem from Title II classification." And Rep. Devin Nunes also objected to the rules.

Rep. Dennis Ross, and Rep. Ryan Zinke, Trump's pick for Interior Secretary, co-sponsored a resolution disapproving the FCC's Open Internet rules. Sen. Jeff Sessions, vice-chair of the transition team and Trump's pick for Attorney General, co-sponsored a senate resolution along the same lines with regard to the 2010 rules.

When the Open Internet Order was challenged in court, both Rep. Blackburn and Rep. Zinke joined a group of House Republicans in an amicus curiae brief to the Court of Appeals for the DC Circuit. The brief argued that the FCC lacked the authority to classify Internet service providers as common carriers under Title II.

Trump's advisor Peter Thiel has likewise been outwardly critical of net neutrality, saying in a Reddit AMA that net neutrality "hasn't been necessary so far, and I'm not sure anything has changed to make it necessary right now. And I don't like government regulation."

It is not yet clear who will be replacing [FCC] Chairman [Tom] Wheeler next year, or who will fill seats vacated by democratic commissioners Jessica Rosenworcel and Mignon Clyburn (when her term ends, or if she decides to leave sooner). Trump has tapped Jeffrey Eisenach, Roslyn Layton and Mark Jamison, three highly vocal opponents of net neutrality, to lead the transition team's work at the agency—suggesting they may be candidates for the post. Eisenach, Layton, and Jamison have all been prolific in their opposition to the FCC's net neutrality rules, and the following merely provide a sample of their comments.

Eisenach, a fellow at the American Enterprise Institute (AEI) and former consultant for Verizon and the trade association GSMA has argued that "net neutrality is not about protecting consumers from rapacious Internet Service Providers (ISPs) … And it has nothing to do with protecting free speech or dissenting voices. Net neutrality is crony capitalism pure and simple—an effort by one group of private interests to enrich itself at the expense of another group by using the power of the state." Eisenach has also called net neutrality a "government mandated rip-off," and a threat to global Internet freedom. In a recent op-ed in the *New York Times*, Eisenach argued "[d]eclaring the Internet a public utility is not necessary, and it will surely prove to be unwise." He's also described it as "a political circus" and "Wheeler's Vietnam."

In 2014, Eisenach testified in Congress and asserted that net neutrality "cannot be justified on grounds of enhancing consumer welfare or protecting the public interest. Rather, it is best understood as an effort by one set of private interests to enrich itself by using the power of the state to obtain free services from another—a classic example of what economists term 'rent seeking.'"

Mark Jamison, a visiting fellow at the SEI and former lobbyist for Sprint, has also been highly critical of the FCC's approach to net neutrality. In an op-ed, Jamison criticized net neutrality as "bestowing benefits to some segments of the industry at the expense of other segments, and at the expense of customers, who ultimately bear the brunt of regulatory rent-seeking." He also called for dramatically scaling back the FCC's duties. He's called the FCC's decision "inconsistent with a stable, evidence-based regulatory approach" and questioned the agency's authority. Jamison has, however, supported a multi-stakeholder best practices approach to net neutrality, or failing that, explicitly Congressionally authorized regulation under limited conditions.

Roslyn Layton, also an AEI fellow, co-authored a report with Jamison, arguing that net neutrality "is failing." Layton also rejects the idea that government regulation is needed to protect net neutrality.

When Trump's administration takes office, the administration will soon be able to appoint three members of the Federal Communications Commission, including a new Chairman. Existing Republican commissioners Ajit Pai and Michael O'Rielly have criticized the commission's net neutrality decision, and dissented from the Commission's Open Internet Order. Either one could also be nominated for the Chairman's position.

Commissioner Pai, in a recent speech, predicted that the Open Internet Order's "days are numbered" and hoped for "a more sober" regulatory approach under the new Administration. In a speech given at the same event, Commissioner O'Rielly expressed a desire to "undo harmful policies" and advised that "[n]ext year's Commission should consider acting quickly to reverse any damaging policies put into place over the last eight years and in the last few weeks of this Administration."

Whoever Trump picks to lead the FCC in the next administration, there's ample reason to believe that net neutrality will be under threat.

> "*The idea that the Internet should be operated like a public "road"— carrying all traffic, with no discrimination against any traveler, no matter what size, shape or type— seems to many a bedrock principle.*"

Net Neutrality Is a Complex Issue

John Wihbey

In the following viewpoint, John Wihbey argues that the issue of net neutrality is far more complex than many who debate it realize. While its supporters maintain that the internet should be available to all, its critics are arguing against government overregulation. The author describes commentary from academics who want to keep the internet open, including commentary from Robin S. Lee and Tim Wu, who originally coined the terminology used today. In the arguments against, the author describes points to research from the Karlsruhe Institute of Technology in Germany, which worries that too much data without regulation will overwhelm the fragile infrastructure of the internet. Wihbey is an assistant professor of journalism and new media at Northeastern University.

As you read, consider the following questions:

1. Per the viewpoint, why should the internet be treated like a public "road"?
2. What do critics of net neutrality claim happens if ISPs are unable to sell faster services to businesses willing to pay?
3. Why do researchers find that the incentive for broadband service providers to expand is higher under net neutrality than if it was abolished?

The Federal Communications Commission (FCC) voted February 26, 2015, in favor of new rules that would enshrine the principle of "net neutrality," with a draft of the "Open Internet Order" then released March 12. This follows a long period of speculation, litigation and political pressure around this issue, stretching back at least five years to the FCC's original open Internet rules.

On Nov. 10, 2014, President Obama announced a new plan to preserve "net neutrality" and to prevent Internet service providers from blocking or slowing websites or creating different tiers of speed. "No service should be stuck in a 'slow lane' because it does not pay a fee," he wrote in a statement. "That kind of gatekeeping would undermine the level playing field essential to the Internet's growth."

The idea that the Internet should be operated like a public "road"—carrying all traffic, with no discrimination against any traveler, no matter what size, shape or type—seems to many a bedrock principle. But should the Internet be regulated like other public utilities—like water or electricity? Under the prior FCC policy, Internet service providers such as Verizon and Comcast (ISPs) had to treat all content equally, including news sites, Facebook and Twitter, cloud-based business activities, role-playing games, Netflix videos, peer-to-peer music file sharing, photos on Flickr—even gambling activity and pornography. Citizens can run all manner of applications and devices, and no content provider is given preferential treatment or a faster "lane" than anyone else. No content can be blocked by Internet service providers or charged differential rates.

But it also meant that ISPs could not sell faster services to businesses willing to pay, a form of market regulation that, critics say, stifles innovation and legitimate commercial activity.

That all data should zip through the "pipes" of the Internet on an equal basis appears to be a natural feature of the system. But this principle of "network neutrality"—a deliberately crafted feature that is enshrined in the FCC's 2010 "Open Internet Order"—has faced major challenges. A lawsuit before the United States Court of Appeals for the District of Columbia Circuit, argued in September 2013, pitted the Federal Communications Commission (FCC) against Verizon. The verdict in the case, delivered January 2014, struck down the FCC's rules.

Verizon and other ISPs have long been able to do "reasonable network management" to keep data and content flowing; what they want is to have more control over traffic and be able to create faster Internet lanes. Some companies assert that net neutrality requirements are unconstitutional, and their elimination will create more business opportunities. Supporters of the network neutrality principle disagree.

The FCC formerly designated the Internet an "information" service, not a "telecommunications" service like telephone companies, and so may not be entitled to regulate the Internet as heavily as it currently does—to oversee an Internet service provider as a "common carrier."

As observers have long pointed out, the issue of net neutrality is often simplified, and in no way is the Internet actually an egalitarian playing field given its current architecture. Companies pay for better server speed; large Internet companies frequently engage in "peering connections," or putting servers in the core architecture of ISPs; and sites and publishers of all kinds pay for content delivery networks (CDNs), which mirror content on servers and speed up delivery (and limit slow load times, or latency.)

What exactly is at stake with the network neutrality principle? What are the broader societal and economic implications? Behind many of the arguments is also a fundamental debate over who should pay for upgrades to and expansion of the current system. Although broadband speeds, price and availability in the United States once ranked high globally, they're now similar to rates in other developed countries, according to OECD. It's an issue news media have begun to pick up.

The Knight Foundation has usefully brought together analysis of various related policy issues and areas of contention and advocacy around the issue. See the December 2014 report "Decoding the Net Neutrality Debate: Media, Public Comment and Advocacy on the Open Internet." And Harvard's Berkman Center for Internet & Society has issued a February 2015 paper exploring how exactly the campaign for net neutrality gathered momentum.

In Support of Net Neutrality

Law professor Susan Crawford, of the Benjamin N. Cardozo School of Law and the Berkman Center, has argued extensively against Verizon's position. Read the amicus brief she co-wrote to support the case of the FCC; it deconstructs many of the arguments currently being advanced for overturning net neutrality.

For a sense of the wider economic reasons to support net neutrality, the paper "Subsidizing Creativity through Network Design: Zero-Pricing and Net Neutrality," published in the *Journal of Economic Perspectives*, provides an overview. The authors, Robin S. Lee of New York University and Tim Wu of Columbia University—who helped coin the term "net neutrality"—look at the innovation possibilities enabled by the Internet and spell out why allowing "termination fees," or costs imposed on content providers to reach customers, would be harmful.

Further, a paper in *Information Systems Research*, "The Debate on Net Neutrality: A Policy Perspective," uses game theory to investigate the potential consequences of the loss of net neutrality. The authors, Hsing Kenneth Cheng and Subhajyoti

OBAMA'S INTERNET

President Barack Obama has called on the Federal Communications Commission to develop new "net neutrality" rules and, equally importantly, establish the legal authority it needs to support those rules by reclassifying broadband service as a "telecommunications service."

This is very welcomed news. Back in May, the Federal Communications Commission proposed flawed "net neutrality" rules that would effectively bless the creation of Internet "slow lanes." After months of netroots protests, we learned the FCC began to settle on a "hybrid" proposal that, we fear, is legally unsustainable.

Here's why: if the FCC is going to craft and enforce clear and limited neutrality rules, it must first do one important thing. The FCC must reverse its 2002 decision to treat broadband as an "information service" rather than a "telecommunications service." This is what's known as Title II reclassification. According to the highest court to review the question, the rules that actually do what many of us want—such as forbidding discrimination against certain applications— require the FCC to treat access providers like "common carriers," treatment that can only be applied to telecommunications services. Having chosen to define broadband as an "information service," the FCC can impose regulations that "promote competition" (good) but it cannot stop providers from giving their friends special access to Internet users (bad).

Today's statement stresses a few key principles:

1. No blocking. If a consumer requests access to a website or service, and the content is legal, your ISP should not be permitted to block it. That way, every player—not just those commercially affiliated with an ISP—gets a fair shot at your business.
2. No throttling.
3. Increased transparency, including with respect to interconnection.
4. No paid prioritization. "No service should be stuck in a 'slow lane' because it does not pay a fee."

> Wisely, the statement explicitly notes the need for forbearance. As we have said for months, reclassification must be combined with a commitment to forbear from imposing aspects of Title II that were originally drafted for 20th century telephone services and that don't make sense for the Internet. While forbearance doesn't set the limits on the regulatory agency in stone, it does require the FCC to make a public commitment that is difficult to reverse.
>
> This is an important moment in the fight for the open Internet.
>
> **"The White House Gets It Right on Net Neutrality. Will the FCC?," by Corynne McSherry, Electronic Frontier Foundation, November 10, 2014.**

Bandyopadhyay of the University of Florida and Hong Guo of the University of Notre Dame, find that ending it would disproportionately favor Internet service providers and hurt content providers. They also find that the "incentive for the broadband service provider to expand under net neutrality is mostly higher than the incentive to expand when the principle of net neutrality is abolished."

A 2014 working paper for the National Bureau of Economic Research, "Weak Versus Strong Net Neutrality," by Joshua Gans of the University of Toronto, support the "notion that strong net neutrality may stimulate content provider investment while the model concludes that there is unlikely to be any negative impact from such regulation on ISP investment. Counter to many claims, it is argued ... that ISP competition may not be a substitute for net neutrality regulation in bringing about these effects."

It should also be noted that a "digital divide" still exists across America, with those of lower socioeconomic status less likely to have broadband access. Thus, any usage-based pricing in local broadband markets might extend this divide beyond mere access and, as former FCC Commissioner Michael Copps has written, potentially make "news and information a luxury good."

Against Strict Neutrality: Counterarguments

Although there is a wealth of scholarship that supports net neutrality, there are also some prominent scholars, such as Christopher Yoo, who argue against taking the mainstream regulatory approach that neutrality supporters prefer. In the 2014 paper "Wickard for the Internet? Network Neutrality After *Verizon v. FCC*," Yoo argues that a new standard based on "commercial reasonableness" may be a better policy direction, and "differentiation of traffic can provide consumer benefits by giving the increasingly heterogeneous universe of consumers a broader array of options from which to choose." He explores underlying and tricky issues of Internet architecture, as well as relevant past legal issues. (Columbia's Wu has had some informative debates with Yoo on these issues.)

A 2013 paper in *Telecommunications Policy*, "Net Neutrality: A Progress Report" analyzes much of the research literature to date. The authors, Jan Kramer, Lukas Wiewiorra and Christof Weinhardt of the Karlsruhe Institute of Technology in Germany, note that given the growth of data traffic on the Internet, there are fears that an "exoflood" of data will ultimately overwhelm the Internet if proper traffic controls are not allowed. Streaming video, such as that from Netflix, constitutes large and growing portions of network traffic. Internet service providers claim that they "cannot bear the costs for the necessary network infrastructure investments without tapping additional revenue streams." The scholars also note that Internet service providers already manage traffic in a variety of ways to ensure what's called "quality of service," and the net neutrality debate sometimes appears to be overly "romantic" and simplistic.

The idea of "strict network neutrality" is thus not realistic; that principle, the authors write, "would imply taking a step backwards from the current status quo of the Internet towards a network regime where any network management practice would be forbidden. Such regulated technical disarming could lead to congestion problems in peak times, which could only be counteracted by overprovisioning of network capacity. In any case, ISPs' revenues would be reduced because business models that rely on managed services, like [Internet television], could not be reliably offered anymore. The likely result of this strict interpretation of [net neutrality] would be that consumer prices for (full) Internet access increase, or that the rate of investments in network infrastructure is reduced."

Kramer, Wiewiorra and Weinhardt review many papers that examine the financial implications of net neutrality, concluding that "the majority of the papers that conduct an economic analysis find that strict [net neutrality] regulation is warranted only under very special circumstances." They also usefully review emerging issues, such as debates over "device neutrality," "search neutrality" and the rise of CDNs and how they are reshaping Web traffic dynamics.

Periodical and Internet Sources Bibliography

The following articles have been selected to supplement the diverse views presented in this chapter.

Association of Community Organizations for Reform Now, Canada, "Internet Use and Accessibility for Low-Income Canadians," ACORN Canada, January 2016. https://www .canadiancontentconsultations.ca/system/file_answers/files /547a94727c2573431ce673b7c15dbce03372a715/001/420/155 /original/Internet_for_All_report_0.pdf?1480100602.

Shahid Buttar, "Net Neutrality Needs You as Much as You Need It," Electronic Frontier Foundation, December 1, 2017. https://www .eff.org/deeplinks/2017/12/net-neutrality-needs-you-much-you -need-it.

Devin Coldewey, "FCC Commissioner Clyburn Guts Anti-net Neutrality Order in Extended Dissent," TechCrunch, January 5, 2018. https://techcrunch.com/2018/01/05/fcc-commissioner -clyburns-extended-dissent-guts-anti-net-neutrality-order/.

Klint Finley, "Tech Giants to Join Legal Battle over Net Neutrality," *Wired*, January 5, 2018. https://www.wired.com/story/tech -giants-to-join-legal-battle-over-net-neutrality/.

Joshua S. Gans, "Weak Versus Strong Net Neutrality," National Bureau of Economic Research, May 2014. http://www.nber.org /papers/w20160.

April Glaser, "Why the FCC Can't Actually Save Net Neutrality," Electronic Frontier Foundation, January 27, 2014. https://www .eff.org/deeplinks/2014/01/why-the-fcc-cant-save-net-neutrality.

John S. and James L. Knight Foundation, "Decoding the Net Neutrality Debate: Media, Public Comment and Advocacy on the Open Internet," Knight Foundation, December 19, 2014. https:// www.issuelab.org/resource/decoding-the-net-neutrality-debate -media-public-comment-and-advocacy-on-the-open-internet .html.

John Kneuer, "Congress Should Ensure Pai's Decision on Net Neutrality Stands Firm," *Hill* (Washington, DC), January 7, 2018. http://thehill.com/opinion/technology/367850-congress-should -ensure-pais-decision-on-net-neutrality-stands-firm.

Jan Kramer, Lukas Wiewiorra, and Christof Weinhardt, "Net Neutrality: A Progress Report," Telecommunications Policy, 2016. http://e-tcs.org/wp-content/uploads/2016/03/Net-neutrality-A -progress-report.pdf.

Robin S. Lee and Tim Wu, "Subsidizing Creativity Through Network Design: Zero Pricing and Net Neutrality," *Journal of Economic Perspectives* 23, no. 3 (2009): 61–76. https://papers.ssrn.com/sol3/papers.cfm?abstract_id= 1489166&rec=1&srcabs=953989&alg=1&pos=4.

Abagail Phillips, "Part I: FCC 'Ancillary' Authority to Regulate the Internet? Don't Count on It," Electronic Frontier Foundation, February 3, 2011. https://www.eff.org/deeplinks/2011/02/part-i -fcc-ancillary-authority-regulate-internet.

Christopher S. Yoo, "*Wickard* for the Internet? Network Neutrality After *Verizon v. FCC*," University of Pennsylvania Law School, 2014. http://scholarship.law.upenn.edu/cgi/viewcontent .cgi?article=2458&context=faculty_scholarship.

OPPOSING
VIEWPOINTS®
SERIES

CHAPTER 2

Should the Internet Be Regulated by the Government?

Chapter Preface

The only easy discussion regarding the internet is knowing that it is incredibly difficult to come to an agreement on how to regulate it. How could it be possible to regulate something that is so expansive, whose boundaries don't necessarily follow the same lines as that of the United States? And if the United States created the internet, shouldn't it be the country that regulates it best?

But the debate lies in the best way to go about protecting those principles, whether it be the rules of the FCC—and it has been long debated whether the FCC has the jurisdiction to enforce rules like that of the 2015 Open Internet Order—or the United States' antitrust laws that have been protecting consumers for decades from predatory business practices.

Though the FCC's 2015 rulings classified broadband access under Title II of the Communications Act, many anti–net neutrality proponents place their concern not in the net neutrality principles themselves but in the potential drawbacks that consumers will one day face if the internet is treated like a utility, which would ultimately place control of the internet in the hands of the federal government. One viewpoint in this chapter poses the idea that removing net neutrality regulations from Title II would actually ensure that the government has no power to censor the internet.

No matter which body regulates the internet, internationally, the consensus is toward laws and rules that protect net neutrality and its principles. Organizations like the United Nations Educational, Scientific and Cultural Organization (UNESCO) and the Body of European Regulations for Electronic Communications (BEREC) place an emphasis on pro–net neutrality regulation as well as the continued spread of access to the internet in not just second- and third-world countries but even among the low-income earners in first-world countries.

> *"The FCC soon found, though, that newly freed broadband providers had an irritating proclivity to block internet services that they didn't like."*

No One Actually Knows How to Regulate the Internet

Justin Fox

In the following viewpoint, Justin Fox argues that regulating the internet in the United States is extremely difficult. He also details how other countries are surpassing the United States in providing net neutrality protections. This leads to questions about what the United States should be doing for internet access, since the internet as it is currently known was born in this country. As the internet has grown from something not often used to something that people feel is a basic necessity, concerns have risen about the best ways to classify it and the growing battle between broadband companies and the cable and phone conglomerates. Fox is a former editorial director of Harvard Business Review *and a columnist for Bloomberg View.*

"No One Actually Knows How to Regulate the Internet," by Justin Fox, Harvard Business School Publishing, November 18, 2014. Reprinted by permission.

As you read, consider the following questions:

1. What were the reasons behind regulatory showdowns between the FCC and broadband providers?
2. Why do cable and phone companies not want broadband providers to be reclassified as telecommunications services?
3. Per the viewpoint, why are other countries surpassing the United States in the Networked Readiness Index?

Here's a little secret: Nobody actually knows what the economic and societal ramifications will be if the Federal Communications Commission heeds President Obama's call to classify broadband internet as a utility (more precisely, a "telecommunications service"). You might be surprised by this if you've been listening for the past week to combatants on both sides declaring with seeming certainty that such a move would either save the internet or ruin it. But it's a little like that saying about academic arguments being so vicious because the stakes are so low—here the convictions are perhaps so strong because the evidence is so inconclusive.

One key reason why the evidence tells us so little is that both sides in the debate can claim, with some justification, that they are just trying to allow the process of creative destruction to keep working its magic. The President is trying to protect the principle, generally known as either "network neutrality" (coined by legal scholar Tim Wu in 2003) or "open internet" (the FCC's favored term for the past few years), that broadband providers shouldn't be allowed to pick winners among the internet companies that use their pipes. His opponents are trying to protect the principle that broadband is a free market (in FCC lingo: an "information service" as opposed to a telecommunications service) in which competition, not government regulation, will bring faster, cheaper internet connections. In both cases, then, the gist of the reasoning is, *It's been going pretty well so far. Why ruin everything?*

A little historical background: In the days of dialup internet service in the 1990s, phone companies were regulated as telecommunications services that had to let internet service providers use their copper wires at reasonable rates, while the ISPs were classified as information services that could do pretty much whatever they wanted. Sure, the biggest ISP, AOL, was constantly trying to pick winners by cutting deals with search engines and content providers, but if you didn't like that there were hundreds of AOL competitors to choose from.

When phone companies started offering faster DSL connections, the FCC determined that these too had to be open to competing ISPs. But when the cable companies jumped in with their even-faster broadband connections the FCC, with Michael Powell (now the chief lobbyist for the cable industry) at the helm, deemed this evidence that competitive forces were working their magic and declared in 2002 that cable broadband was an information service that didn't have to let other ISPs piggyback on its pipes. After a few years of legal wrangling, the Commission extended this status to the phone companies' broadband offerings. Since then the US has relied mainly on competition between local-monopoly telcos and local-monopoly cable companies to spark investment and protect consumers.

The FCC soon found, though, that newly freed broadband providers had an irritating proclivity to block internet services that they didn't like. The first showdown was with Madison River Communications, a North Carolina telephone company that was blocking Vonage voice-over-internet calls. In 2005 the FCC ordered it to stop. A couple years later it was Comcast blocking BitTorrent and other peer-to-peer file-sharing services for using up too much bandwidth. The FCC ruled in 2008 that such behavior "unduly squelches the dynamic benefits of an open and accessible internet." Comcast sued, and an appellate court ruled that since Comcast was supposed to be a lightly regulated information service, the FCC didn't have legal authority to do that. The FCC issued a revised "open internet" rule, Verizon sued, and the

Pai Draws Ire

FCC Chairman Ajit Pai will visit the Bay Area, supposedly for a "fireside chat" with tech executives about bridging the digital divide for underserved communities. But Chairman Pai's brief tenure to this point has been defined by actions that undermine digital rights, such as seeking to rescind the Open Internet Order of 2015 that protects net neutrality via light touch regulations to ensure equal opportunity online.

Since Mr. Pai's appointment in January by President Trump, their lobbyists have flooded the agency and the offices of Congress, pushing for an unwinding of rules that they say hamper their businesses …

Mr. Pai has been an active figure in the Trump administration's quest to dismantle regulations. He froze a broadband subsidy program for low-income households, eased limits on television station mergers and eased caps on how much a company like AT&T or Comcast can charge another business to get online.

Pai's appearance in San Francisco will prompt protest, as his proposal is overwhelmingly opposed by the public, including both Democrats and Republicans. Outside the location at which he'll meet with tech executives, EFF and a number of allied organizations (including the Center for Media Justice, ACLU of Northern California, The Greenlining Institute, CREDO, 18 Million Rising, the Media Alliance, Tech Workers Coalition, and more) will host a rally to which all are welcome.

The Center for Media Justice put it bluntly: "Our communities depend on a free and open internet to innovate, organize for racial justice, and communicate. With people of color, queer and trans folks, and other marginalized communities at risk, our fight for democracy depends on our ability to connect with one another without censorship or interference."

The Internet has developed into a diverse and innovative platform thanks in large part to the requirement that Internet providers treat data equally, without discriminating between data from one source versus another. This neutrality has been a defining cornerstone of the Internet's architecture since its early days.

> Both innovation and dissent rely on Internet users—not the company providing them bandwidth—being in control over what they read and say online. If those companies are allowed to play favorites, or to hold their customers hostage to demand tolls from those who want to reach them, opportunities for both job creation and meaningful dissent will predictably wither.
>
> The fight to save net neutrality will take all of us.
>
> "FCC Chair's 'Chat' with Tech Execs Draws Protest," by Shahid Buttar, Electronic Frontier Foundation, September 11, 2017.

same appellate court ruled again that the FCC didn't have legal authority to do that. This is why the FCC is again revising its open internet rules and considering reclassifying broadband providers as telecommunications services to make its authority clearer, and why the President has urged the Commission to do so.

The cable and phone companies really, really, really don't want this to happen. But it is of course they who have driven the FCC to this point. Comcast executive vice president David L. Cohen claimed the other day that his company agrees with all four of the open-internet principles espoused by President Obama. But the company has had a funny way of showing that—suing the FCC when it tried to enforce those principles in the past and, when the latest open internet rules were thrown out in court early this year, immediately cutting a deal with Netflix that sure seems to be a direct violation of Obama's fourth principle ("No paid prioritization"). The sheer disingenuousness of the cable industry's spokespeople is a remarkable thing to behold.

That disingenuousness, while it should lead us to take every industry statement with a big bucket of rock salt, does not on its own settle the debate over whether switching its regulatory status is a great idea or a terrible one. But for this we can at least look to some evidence: Almost every other affluent country on earth already does regulate broadband provision as a utility. Most of them also have faster broadband connections, higher broadband penetration, and lower prices than the US does. It's not clear there's a cause-and-effect relationship here (more on that in a moment), but it is apparent that more regulation doesn't necessarily spell internet stagnation. That's partly because the standard approach to regulating monopolies has moved on since the 1930s (thanks in part to the work of this year's economics Nobel laureate, Jean Tirole). Rather than restricting the prices that broadband providers charge consumers, overseas regulators have for the most part tried instead to foster competition by forcing telephone and/or cable companies to unbundle their services and/or share parts of their networks with other internet service providers—as the FCC did before 2002.

The FCC hasn't done that for the past 12 years, and the results relative to other rich nations have been, as noted above, below average. Given the vast physical size of this country and the way its population is dispersed, this isn't as terrible as it sounds (denser populations deliver higher returns on broadband investment). But the US, as the birthplace of the internet, started out way ahead in internet access, and since 2002 South Korea and several Northern European countries have blown past it. The US scores better in rankings that emphasize business connectivity, like the World Economic Forum's Networked Readiness Index. But even there we've lost ground—from third place in 2008–2009 to seventh this year.

While almost all the countries that rank above the US in broadband penetration have some sort of open-access regulation, economic studies of the link between regulation and broadband access have often concluded that open-access rules depress investment. Without the prospect of monopoly profits, the reasoning goes, telcos and cable companies have less incentive to invest. But this isn't the only view. An exhaustive 2009 roundup by researchers at Harvard's Berkman Center for Internet and Society found the 38 multi-country economic studies of broadband regulation and investment they looked at to be hopelessly split between positive, negative, and inconclusive results. The Berkman researchers also argued that we shouldn't pay too much heed to the economists because (1) a lot of the studies were sponsored by broadband incumbents, (2) there simply isn't enough data yet for the empirical surveys to be trusted, and (3) different theoretical models of broadband investment deliver dramatically different results. The Berkmanites advised looking instead at qualitative case studies of the countries with the highest broadband penetration, which generally show regulators playing an active role in encouraging and enabling competition. But these countries also tend to be smallish, well-governed, and willing to invest significant taxpayer resources in broadband, so it's not clear to me that it's the open-access rules per se that have driven broadband success—or if a sprawling, politically polarized, endlessly litigious country with a distrust of public infrastructure investment is going to struggle to keep up with nimbler rivals in its broadband rollout regardless of its regulatory approach.

Where does that leave us? The US is a broadband laggard, or at best a broadband also-ran. The current regulatory debate doesn't really address that, though. Instead, it's all about the ability of internet companies (and non-profits, and individuals) to reach consumers (or, more broadly, an audience) without Comcast or Verizon charging them a toll or picking favorites. Despite its less-than-blisteringly fast broadband connections, the US is home to the most vibrant internet sector on the planet, so something about the way things have evolved here over the past couple of decades has definitely worked. My take is that this something is a combination of the fact that the internet started here (as a government project, of course), Silicon Valley's pre-internet experience with launching new companies and industries and disrupting old ones, and the open architecture of the internet—not so much the regulatory status of the broadband providers. But it's also possible that competitive forces and the FCC can keep that open architecture largely intact even if the Commission doesn't decide that broadband is a utility. The most recent appeals court ruling pointed a way to doing that, which the FCC tried to follow in its initial rule proposal in May, which unleashed torrents of pro-net-neutrality outrage, which has brought us to where we are now. Whichever path the FCC chooses to follow next, you can be sure that somebody will sue, and the matter will end up being decided by federal judges, possibly the Supremes. Did I mention that this is an endlessly litigious country?

Lots of things are possible. The future is uncertain. If either side in the net neutrality debate could just admit that, I think it'd be a huge step forward.

> "For UNESCO, effective press
> freedom is based on media freedom,
> pluralism, independence and safety."

Freedom of Expression
Includes a Free Internet

UNESCO

The following viewpoint is an excerpt from a four-part report on the impact of media development on freedom of expression. It was released by the United Nations Educational, Scientific and Cultural Organization (UNESCO), and it acknowledges the impact the internet and digital media have on its two definitions of freedom of expression, which are crucial to the growth of free and open societies. Along with studying the connection between freedom of expression and digital technologies, the excerpt also describes the six points of research within the UNESCO Series of Internet Freedom, as set forth in the 2013 Resolution 52 by the General Conference. UNESCO is a specialized agency of the United Nations focusing on education, science, and culture.

"World Trends in Freedom of Expression and Media Development: Special Digital Focus 2015," UNESCO Publications. http://unesdoc.unesco.org/images/0023/002349/234933e.pdf. Licensed under CC-BY-SA 3.0 IGO.

As you read, consider the following questions:

1. In what ways does the internet impact UNESCO's two dimensions of freedom of expression?
2. Did the *Keystones* study find a connection between freedom of expression and new technologies?
3. What does the viewpoint state are some of the hurdles freedom of expression faces with the expansion of available digital technology?

UNESCO is the UN agency with a mandate to defend freedom of expression, instructed by its Constitution to promote "the free flow of ideas by word and image." This mission is reinforced by the Universal Declaration of Human Rights, which affirms, "Everyone has the right to freedom of opinion and expression." Freedom of expression, and its corollaries of freedom of information and press freedom, applies to all media, including traditional print and broadcast media, as well as newer digital media.

In 2013, UNESCO's General Conference of 195 Member States adopted Resolution 52, which recalled Human Rights Council Resolution A/HRC/RES/20/8, "The Promotion, Protection and Enjoyment of Human Rights on the Internet" [...] This current study continues the mandate, and uses the conceptual framework of the first World Trends report, which highlights issues of freedom, pluralism, independence, safety and gender. Also informing the current study is the mandate of the 37th General Conference in 2013, where Resolution 52 called for a comprehensive and consultative study of four dimensions of the internet as relevant to the remit of UNESCO. Published as *Keystones to foster inclusive Knowledge Societies*, that study examined access to information and knowledge, freedom of expression, privacy and the ethical dimensions of the information society.

Building on this background, UNESCO recognises that as digital technologies become ever more central to societies, so the issues around online freedom of expression, and its interface with the off-line world, also call for attention by the Organization. An example here is the safety of journalists and the issue of impunity, which is one of the chapters in this World Trends report. What happens in this realm in the practical world has a major bearing on what happens in the online dimensions—and vice versa. A lack of safety in one sphere has repercussions for safety in the other sphere.

[...]

The first dimension of free expression is the right to impart information and opinion. This is the foundation for the right to press freedom, which refers to the freedom to publish to a wider audience. In the digital age, this right is especially relevant to anyone who uses traditional or social media. For UNESCO, effective press freedom is based on media freedom, pluralism, independence and safety. This applies to all media, including creative media and social media, and not just to the news media. Within this perspective, the matter of independence is of special relevance to those who use press freedom to do journalism. Independence depends on freedom and pluralism, and in the case of journalism, whether online or off-line, and this is founded upon the existence of professional standards for the production and circulation of verifiable information in the public interest.

In a nutshell, freedom of expression is the parent of press freedom—understood as the use of the right to impart information on a mass scale. Media freedom, pluralism, independence and safety constitute the essential enabling environment for the exercise of press freedom. It is within this context that professional journalism, as an offspring of freedom of expression, can flourish and make its contribution to building knowledge societies.

The second dimension of freedom of expression is the right to seek and receive information, which is the foundation of the right to information. In turn, this is one of the foundations of transparency, which is recognised as essential for development and democracy. Huge advances in transparency are enabled by digital technologies, as regards both public and private institutions, allowing for unprecedented accountability and citizen empowerment.

These two dimensions of freedom of expression are increasingly intertwined with the right to privacy, with potential synergies as well as tensions. Strong privacy can strengthen the ability of journalism to draw on confidential sources for public interest information, but it can also weaken transparency and conceal information in which there could be legitimate public interest. Weak privacy can lead to journalistic sources withholding information or practising self-censorship because of a fear of being arbitrarily monitored. Weak privacy may also enable an over-reach in transparency, amounting to an unjustified intrusion into individuals' personal lives. Trust in the benefits of digital communications can be affected by how a society addresses the right to privacy with the two dimensions of the right to freedom of expression.

Much of the work of UNESCO provides insight into how the two rights can each be respected, online as well as off-line—and where these interface, as well as how they can be balanced harmoniously in the public interest where necessary. The Organization does this through providing research, monitoring, awareness raising, advocacy, capacity building, and technical advice. UNESCO's International Programme for the Development of Communication (IPDC) also provides grant support for relevant projects for free, pluralistic, independent and secure media, whether online or off-line.

At the standard-setting level of defending online freedom of expression and privacy, UNESCO has actively been involved in and contributed to global and regional processes, including the NETmundial Internet Governance Principles and Roadmap for the future evolution of the Internet governance, the Council of Europe's Recommendation on Internet freedom, the African Declaration on Internet Rights and Freedoms, and the European Union's Seventh Framework Programme's project on "Managing Alternatives for Privacy, Property and Internet Governance."

[…]

As per the mandate, UNESCO produced the study by convening an inclusive multistakeholder process which included governments, private sector, civil society, international organizations and the technical community. In July 2014, an online questionnaire was launched and inputs were solicited through social media and major fora, as well as directly sought from Member States and more than 300 experts and organizations, representing civil society, academia, the private sector, the technical community and intergovernmental organizations. By the end [of] November 2014, UNESCO had received 200 solid responses to the questionnaire. Input to the study was also sought at global fora on internet-related issues, and a thematic debate on online freedom of expression and privacy was held at the 29th meeting of the Council of the IPDC in November 2014. In parallel to the multistakeholder consultations, UNESCO commissioned a series of publications on specific sub-themes to provide in-depth analysis and recommendations to its Member States and other stakeholders on internet freedom issues. These sub-studies contributed to the wider internet study, with some also being published as stand-alone volumes in the flagship Series on Internet Freedom.

In addition to the sub-studies that have also contributed to three chapters in this present publication (i.e., *Countering Online Hate Speech*, *Protecting Journalism Sources in the Digital Age*, and *Fostering Freedom Online: The Role of Internet Intermediaries*), UNESCO has also commissioned a wide range of research within the framework of the Series on Internet Freedom, in the context of the 2013 Resolution 52 by the General Conference:

1. Building Digital Safety for Journalism: A Survey of Selected Issues

In light of limited global understanding of emerging safety threats linked to digital developments, UNESCO commissioned this research within the Organization's on-going efforts to implement the UN Plan of Action on the Safety of Journalists and the Issue of Impunity. In examining cases worldwide, the publication serves as a resource for a range of actors by surveying evolving threats and assessing preventive, protective and pre-emptive measures. It shows that digital security for journalism encompasses, but also goes beyond, the technical dimension. Recommendations are proposed for consideration by Member States, regarding governments, journalism contributors and sources, news organizations, trainers, corporations and international organizations.

2. Principles for Governing the Internet: A Comparative Analysis

This research reviews more than 50 internet-specific declarations and frameworks relevant to internet principles, prompted by a need for a specific review of the declarations and frameworks from the perspective of UNESCO's mandate. The publication shows that while each of these documents has its own value, none of them fully align with UNESCO's priorities and mandate. It there puts forward for Member States' consideration the concept of "Internet Universality" as the Organization's clear identifier for approaching the various fields of internet issues and their intersections with UNESCO concerns. This concept has relevance to the Organization's work in many areas—including online freedom of expression and privacy; efforts to advance universality in education, social inclusion and gender equality; multilingualism in cyberspace; access to information and knowledge; and ethical dimensions of information society.

3. Online Licensing and Free Expression

UNESCO commissioned research on the topic of online licensing and free expression, particularly as regards journalism. Restricting access to using a means of communication is a matter directly related to press freedom; it has emerged as a complimentary approach to the longer standing practices of filtering and blocking, which impact particularly on the right to seek and receive information. From the point of view of international standards, free expression is the norm and restrictions the exception. When registration serves as licensing in the sense of being both compulsory and exclusionary, it may be seen as a form of prior restraint. Therefore, strict tests are needed to ensure that registration can be justified by the international standards of necessity, proportionality, due process and legitimate purpose. The purpose of this research is to provide contemporary and evidence-based answers to questions around the issue of by-permission publishing online that have been raised by recent policy, legal and regulatory regimes.

4. Privacy and Media and Information Literacy

UNESCO is conducting global research into privacy and media and information literacy (MIL). The issue of internet users having MIL competencies about the different dimensions of privacy is explored, such as public awareness of privacy rights in cyberspace, including national data protection regimes; ability to evaluate how privacy is respected in digital content and communication that is accessed by a user; and ability to evaluate legitimate limitations of privacy online. The research seeks data on these areas, both by marshalling publicly available data in specific countries and regions, and by analysis of MIL practice in the same areas.

5. Balancing Privacy and Transparency

UNESCO commissioned global research on balancing privacy with transparency, the latter being assessed in terms of its relationship to freedom of expression. The research unpacks the complexity of the subject through both normative and empirical information, extending analysis to actors across individuals, civil society, private sector and government. The issue of user trust in the belief that personal data will not be illegitimately rendered transparent is also covered. Risks to personal privacy from transparency will be outlined, as are risks to transparency from privacy. There will be analysis of cases showing the issues and the lessons arising. Good practices in reconciling privacy and transparency are identified in terms of their correspondence with international standards.

6. Privacy and Encryption

This study discusses the availability of different means of encryption and their possible applications, providing a short overview of the state of the art in encryption technologies deployed in the internet and communications industries. It analyses the relationship between encryption and human rights, at the international level including relevant cases at national levels. The study provides an overview of legal developments with respect to government restrictions on encryption in selected jurisdictions and reviews options on encryption policy at the international level, including ideas for enhancing "encryption literacy."

Through the multi-stakeholder consultation and the sub-studies, UNESCO identified the four fields of research as being interdependent building blocks for the internet. Published as *Keystones to foster inclusive Knowledge Societies*, the study underlined the widespread interest in a future for the internet as an open, trusted and global resource that is equally accessible to all across the world. It analysed issues for technology and policy providing support greater and more equitable access to information and knowledge, for strengthening freedom of expression as an instrument of democratic processes and accountability, and for reinforcing the privacy of personal information.

The *Keystones* study found that freedom of expression is not an inevitable result of new technologies. Rather, freedom of expression must be supported by policy and practice, and requires trust in the internet as a safe channel for expressing one's views. Rising concerns over surveillance and internet filtering, for example, have led to the perception of freedom of expression on the internet becoming threatened, requiring major efforts to instil trust in privacy, security and the authenticity of information and knowledge accessible online, and to protect the safety and dignity of journalists, social media users and those imparting information and opinion online.

Moreover, *Keystones* established that freedom of expression online is linked to the principle of openness, particularly in regard to the international standards that advocate transparency in relation to restrictions on the right to expression. Open opportunities to share ideas and information on the internet are integral to UNESCO's work to promote freedom of expression, media pluralism and intercultural dialogue. For UNESCO, freedom of expression online is also a question of how people use their access to the internet and related ICTs to express themselves. Media and information literacy for all men and women is relevant to this question, including youth engagement and the countering of all forms of hatred, racism and discrimination, as well as violent extremism, in digital contexts, ranging from email to online video games.

To discuss the draft of the *Keystones* study, UNESCO organized a conference on "CONNECTing the Dots: Options for Future Action," with some 400 participants representing five continents, at UNESCO headquarters in Paris in March 2015. The event provided a platform for exploring the findings of the study in preparation for its finalisation and featured presentations by a wide range of speakers from around the world. With overwhelming agreement, the multi-stakeholder gathering adopted an Outcome Document that underscored the significance of the internet for human progress and its role in fostering inclusive knowledge societies. The Outcome Document affirms the human rights principles that underpin UNESCO's approach to internet-related issues, and supports the Internet Universality principles that promote a Human **R**ights–based, **O**pen internet, which is **A**ccessible to all and characterized by **M**ultistakeholder participation (R.O.A.M). The *Keystones* analysis is that the four principles provide the guiding logic for supporting the further development of the internet in ways that will enhance access to information and knowledge, freedom of expression, privacy and ethics.

A resolution adopted by UNESCO's 196th Executive Board in April 2015 recommended that the Outcome Document of the CONNECTing the Dots conference be considered by the 38th session of the General Conference and forwarded as a non-binding input to the post-2015 Development Agenda; the UN

General Assembly overall WSIS review process; and the high-level meeting of the General Assembly established by General Assembly Resolution 68/302. This Outcome Document is reflected in the options for future action, as outlined in the *Keystones* study.

[…]

Through cutting-edge research and contributions to multi-stakeholder dialogue, UNESCO has thus engaged across the board, with the intention of strengthening the fundamental rights of freedom of expression and privacy, across online and off-line realms, within the ever-deepening digital age.

> *"Title II subjects regulated entities to significant government oversight regarding what services they must offer, to whom, and at what rates."*

Title II Should Not Be Confused with Net Neutrality

Daniel Lyons

In the following viewpoint, Daniel Lyons argues that removing internet providers from Title II actually reduces the risk of government censorship of the internet and further allows for the infrastructure to expand to allow for internet access to continue in the manner that current users expect. Additionally, Lyons's viewpoint asserts that FCC commissioner Ajit Pai intends to protect the principles of net neutrality without the so-called baggage that comes from regulating the internet under Title II. Lyons is a visiting fellow at the American Enterprise Institute, where he focuses on telecommunications and internet regulation.

"A Win for the Internet: The FCC Wants to Repeal Title II Net Neutrality Regulations," by Daniel Lyons, American Enterprise Institute, April 26, 2017. Reprinted by permission.

As you read, consider the following questions:

1. What was Title II of the Communications Act originally intended to regulate?
2. Per the viewpoint, how does repealing net neutrality ultimately benefit online privacy?
3. How does the removal of net neutrality protections under Title II benefit infrastructure investment?

Earlier today, Federal Communications Commission (FCC) Chairman Ajit Pai proposed that the agency repeal its 2015 decision to reclassify broadband providers as common carriers under Title II of the Communications Act. His announcement will likely meet significant opposition from net neutrality advocates, who have long tried to confuse these separate issues. It is worth pausing to explain precisely what Title II is and how it differs from net neutrality (the idea that broadband providers should treat all internet traffic the same and not favor some content over others). Even some net neutrality proponents recognize that repealing Title II will be a boon to the internet ecosystem.

Repealing Title II Would Mean Broadband Providers Are No Longer Subject to Outdated Public Utility Regulations

Congress passed Title II back in the 1930s. Forget the internet—this was before most Americans had television. Modeled on 19th-century railroad regulations, the original purpose of Title II was to rein in the old Bell Telephone monopoly. In its full glory, Title II subjects regulated entities to significant government oversight regarding what services they must offer, to whom, and at what rates. While this regulatory model may be appropriate for static utility monopolies such as water delivery, it is inappropriate in a competitive, dynamic market such as internet access. Companies must be able to adapt quickly to meet competitive challenges and provide new goods and services. Common carriage obligations make it difficult for companies to do so by holding out an ever-present threat of regulatory interference to thwart innovation.

In fact, most traditional common carriage industries—including airlines, trucking, electricity, and even telephones—have long been retreating from the public utility model. In that sense, the Obama FCC's reclassification decision was a big step backward, in many senses of the word.

Repealing Title II Clarifies the Law in Areas Such as Online Privacy

Admittedly, the FCC has voluntarily "forbeared" from applying the most stringent parts of Title II to broadband providers, such as rate regulation. This is because the Obama-era FCC did not truly believe broadband providers were public utilities like the Bell monopoly; it sought Title II reclassification merely as a means to enact net neutrality rules. But the effect was akin to fitting square pegs into round holes, as the FCC used Title II in ways Congress never intended. Because the law was an imperfect fit, it led to significant gaps and confusion that made regulation worse rather than better.

The recent online privacy debate is an excellent example of this. Before 2015, the Federal Trade Commission (FTC) had long been the "cop on the beat" for privacy issues, both offline and online. But one of the unintended consequences of the FCC's reclassification order was to strip the FTC of jurisdiction over broadband providers, as the FTC cannot regulate common carriers. The FCC could have filled this void by simply applying the FTC's rules to broadband providers. Instead, it adopted a more stringent regime, creating an uneven playing field where competing companies were subject to different rules imposed by different regulators. This unfairness led Congress to repeal the FCC's privacy rule, leaving broadband providers again unregulated.

Repealing Title II would strip broadband providers of the common carrier designation and restore FTC jurisdiction over their privacy practices. This would once again unite privacy law

"A Solution in Search of a Problem"

In an interview that year [2015], then-FCC commissioner Ajit Pai called net neutrality "a solution in search of a problem." Instead, he said, policies should focus on bringing greater competition to the American broadband marketplace.

Now, Pai is the newly appointed chairman of the FCC, and his perspective has some wondering what net neutrality might look like in this administration. In a press conference after his first FCC meeting as chairman, Pai told reporters, "I favor a free and open internet, and I oppose Title II."

Jon Brodkin covered the January FCC meeting for Ars Technica. "I don't think unregulated entirely is what he wants," he says. "But he wants to eliminate the Title II classification, which … requires internet providers to be just and reasonable in their practices and rates. And by getting rid of that, that would also get rid of the net neutrality rules."

Brodkin explains the lack of competition: While it's illegal for a city to give exclusive contracts to cable companies, "that doesn't mean that there has to be multiple companies," he says. "Ultimately, it's the decision of private providers as to whether it's worth going into a city or town."

He describes sole internet providers in an area as "de facto" monopolies, not legal monopolies. "Because when Comcast controls the customers in a city or town, it's just not financially feasible for another provider to come in."

In February, the FCC dropped an investigation into a practice known as "zero-rating"—when mobile carriers and internet providers don't count traffic from certain content or services towards customers' data caps. As Brodkin explains in ArsTechnica, questions were raised about zero-rating because carriers like AT&T and Verizon can use it to promote their own video-streaming services, "while charging other video providers for the same data cap exemptions."

"The prior FCC said that AT&T's sponsored data plan, which is that zero-rating kind of plan, looked like it was not lawful under the existing open internet rules," [Susan] Crawford says. "They did that in a report issued right before the Pai FCC came in. And Pai has

> now pulled that report off the table, along with a report saying that investment in infrastructure by government is a really good idea."
>
> For Crawford, there's a clear pattern in the new chairman's approach to internet regulation. "Pai is interested in just helping the existing carriers do whatever they want."
>
> **"What Could Happen to Net Neutrality Under the New FCC?," by Julia Franz, Public Radio International, March 9, 2017.**

under one regulator, a regulator with vast experience overseeing privacy issues and with a clear understanding of how privacy law affects policies throughout the internet ecosystem.

Repealing Title II Reduces the Risk of Future Government Mischief and Likely Boosts Infrastructure Investment

While the FCC is currently forbearing from applying Title II's most draconian measures, there is no guarantee that future commissioners will continue to honor this self-imposed limitation. At any moment, the agency could conclude that forbearance is no longer appropriate and subject regulated entities to rate regulation, tariffing, and a host of other public utility requirements. In this legal regime, Title II hangs as a sword of Damocles over the broadband industry, generating uncertainty, limiting innovation, and likely reducing capital investment in the sector. This makes it more difficult for broadband providers to build the networks needed to close the digital divide, because of fear that these networks will be subjected to unclear future regulatory mandates. Repealing Title II alleviates that anxiety and should restore capital investment to pre-2015 levels.

Repealing Title II Does Not Eliminate Net Neutrality

Finally, contrary to the claims of many advocates, repealing Title II does not necessarily mean the elimination of net neutrality.

Before 2015, the DC Circuit Court offered the FCC a path to enact net neutrality rules without using Title II. A bipartisan Congress also offered to adopt the rules by statute. The Obama-era FCC rejected these compromise measures, but they remain on the table. While they may not regulate broadband providers as completely as Title II, they do allow the agency to enforce core net neutrality principles: that broadband providers should not be able to block or unreasonably discriminate against lawful internet content. Chairman Pai seeks to protect these principles, without the additional baggage that comes from Title II.

> *"Part of [Pai's] argument against net neutrality is that reversing it will make expansion easier for smaller internet providers, who'll have more time and money to focus on infrastructure."*

Net Neutrality Destroys Small ISPs

Jacob Kastrenakes

In the following viewpoint, Jacob Kastrenakes argues that the smaller ISPs have played an outsized role in the net neutrality debate. As many anti-net neutrality arguments focus on the concerns that it will stifle these small companies' abilities to expand and could potentially damage the infrastructure of the internet, the reality is that many small ISPs agree with aspects of these rules, including the core tenets: no blocking websites, no throttling internet speeds, no demanding payments for access. Kastrenakes also points out the financial hurdles these ISPs face but notes the classification of a "small" ISP has grown to protect more companies from financial strain. Kastrenakes is Circuit Breaker *editor at the* Verge.

"The FCC Says Net Neutrality Destroys Small ISPs. So Has It?," by Jacob Kastrenakes, Vox Media, Inc., July 13, 2017. Reprinted by permission.

As you read, consider the following questions:

1. What were the hurdles placed in front of small ISPs toward expansion following the addition of net neutrality rules?

2. Why would small ISPs be in favor of net neutrality regulations?

3. What do ISPs fear may happen if the FCC continues on its path of deregulating the ISP industry?

Net neutrality is meant to prevent internet giants like Comcast, Verizon, and AT&T from wielding their huge networks as weapons to suppress competition from web companies like Netflix, Dropbox, and even sources of news. While those large ISPs account for the vast majority of US internet subscribers, there are thousands of other internet providers out there that don't have that kind of power. And though they're small, they've played an outsized role in the net neutrality debate.

In April [2017], 22 small cable providers signed a letter to the Federal Communications Commission asking for the end of net neutrality, writing that the policy imposed "onerous burdens" on their businesses. FCC chairman Ajit Pai has latched onto this. Since he was named chairman in January, he's been touting the damage net neutrality could do to regional and "mom and pop" internet providers, and he cited this letter as proof when announcing plans to reverse net neutrality and its classification of internet providers under a legal statute known as Title II.

"Heavy-handed regulations are especially tough on new entrants and small businesses that don't have the armies of lawyers and compliance officers that large, well-established companies do," Pai said just one day later. "So if we want to encourage smaller competitors to enter into the broadband marketplace or expand, we must end Title II."

These ISPs are by and large quite small. They include regional cable and telephone companies, municipal broadband providers, and fixed wireless internet companies that deliver service to the home. On the larger side of things are urban internet providers like Sonic, which serves around 100,000 subscribers throughout California. On the smaller side are the wireless providers, which get particularly tiny. One company, Grand County Internet Services, which operates in Colorado about 60 miles outside Denver, is run by two people—a father–daughter team—and has just 1,000 customers.

Quite a few of these smaller internet providers have taken issue with the FCC's net neutrality rules. This is not because of the rules' core tenets—no blocking websites, no throttling internet speeds, no demanding payments for access—which many small providers say they support. Instead, they're concerned about being forced to spend tens of thousands of dollars proving to the FCC that they're actually following the rules.

The Verge called eight smaller internet providers to find out whether they'd been impacted by net neutrality, and the answers were mixed. Multiple respondents, when asked if Title II was hurting them, gave an unqualified "no." Mark Jen, the chief technical officer of a small internet provider in California named Common, which was founded last year by a group of former Square employees, said that complying with net neutrality doesn't require any work.

"The default configuration of all of the [networking] equipment is to [follow net neutrality]," Jen says. "While net neutrality sounds like rules and regulations, it's actually just saying everybody has to run stuff in the default mode, which is as fast as possible and great for everybody."

Rudy Rucker, co-founder of another small wireless internet provider in California, named Monkeybrains, said his company hadn't encountered any difficulties either. "Maybe there's something I'm missing," he said, "but it's not bogging us down."

On the other hand, Elizabeth Bowles, who runs the five-person ISP division of Aristotle, which provides internet access to several thousand people in Central Arkansas, has been an outspoken critic.

"I don't believe that small businesses were the target of the Open Internet Order," says Bowles. "I believe that it was a byproduct casualty of the Open Internet Order that the FCC didn't adequately take into account."

Bowles, who also chairs the legislative committee for the Wireless Internet Service Providers Association and has testified before Congress on its behalf, believes Rucker and the other small ISPs that aren't concerned with net neutrality are missing something. "There is a lack of education among a lot of the small [wireless internet service providers], and they believe that if they meet the bright-line rules, then they've met the requirements," Bowles says, referring to the no blocking, throttling, and paid prioritization rules. "And they haven't."

Bowles points to a series of reporting requirements that force internet providers to disclose network performance, data caps, and other network statistics to the FCC. While doing that might seem as simple as clicking a few buttons on a computer, Bowles says that wireless ISPs estimated a cost of $40,000 per year to deal with these reports. Those costs would come from engineers, writers, and outside counsel, as well as software costs, according to congressional testimony she gave last year.

But right after the Open Internet Order was passed, the FCC temporarily removed those reporting requirements from internet providers with fewer than 100,000 subscribers. And at the beginning of this year, the exemption was expanded to providers with fewer than 250,000 subscribers and prolonged for five more years. With the requirements lifted, Bowles says that those estimated costs largely disappear. Though she points out the reporting exemption is "still temporary."

Nathan Stooke, the CEO of Wisper, a wireless internet provider in southern Illinois, has other concerns with the net neutrality rules. When they were created, the FCC opened up the ability for anyone to file a complaint with the commission about possible rule violations—and internet providers can be required to respond to them.

"We have to use reasonable efforts to get a customer serviced" under Title II, Stooke says. "Well, whose definition of 'reasonable?' … One of our customers now has been a customer for 13 years, and we can't get her good, reliable service. With our fixed wireless, the trees have grown up between the power she gets services from and her house. And she said, 'Well, I read on the FCC website, under Title II, you're required to give me service.' Well, okay, yes, but I physically can't."

Stooke, whose company has 72 employees and serves about 13,000 subscribers, says the complaint line isn't necessary for small providers—he'll hear the complaints straight from his customers. "I go to church with my customers. I go to the grocery store and see my customers," he says. "They let me know when I'm not doing a very good job and not providing a good service."

Eden Recor, who runs Grand County Internet Services, said he had the same concern. "I have had a couple customers in the past years … because of the way the trees were around their houses, we could not get service in there," he said. "And they reported us to the Better Business Bureau and raised all sorts of havoc."

Three of the internet providers we spoke with had received complaints, but none that presented such an impasse. Aristotle received one regarding a bandwidth problem. Wisper received two and said the FCC was "very helpful" with one of them. Monkeybrains received a complaint after shutting off service for someone who hadn't paid their bill in nine months. "The FCC handled the issue very well," a Monkeybrains representative said in an email. "We provided evidence of their usage and financial delinquency, and the case was closed."

The FCC estimates that it should only take internet providers 15 minutes to respond to a complaint that gets passed along to them. And not all complaints actually make it through—some just end up with a pat response from the FCC.

Gigi Sohn, who was an advisor to former FCC chairman Tom Wheeler when the net neutrality rules were drafted and passed, said in an email that it seems to her that some wireless internet providers are "spinning themselves up and dreaming up worst case scenarios that will never come to pass."

"It isn't going to happen, and if it did, the FCC would dismiss the complaint out of hand," she writes. "The FCC doesn't act on every complaint—just those that make a prima facie case that the rules have been broken. So it really isn't a reasonable concern."

Internet providers big and small have broadly blamed uncertainties in how the net neutrality rules will be applied, causing them to halt expansions of their businesses. But it's not clear how much that's happened. Recor says, "I can't stop expanding and maintain my customer base."

The expansion of smaller ISPs has been a sticking point for Pai. He's repeatedly come back to this topic, making support for rural broadband a focus of his chairmanship, as it's these smaller companies that often reach communities that aren't yet wired up. Part of his argument against net neutrality is that reversing it will make expansion easier for smaller internet providers, who'll have more time and money to focus on infrastructure. If net neutrality is hurting their expansion, then it's also hurting a major FCC goal: seeing that all Americans can get online.

During his speech announcing the reversal of Title II, Pai cited part of Bowles' 2016 congressional testimony, in which she said that Aristotle had "pulled back" on plans to triple its customer base and instead decided to make several smaller deployments instead. But now Bowles says the plan to triple the company's customer base is moving forward once again. "We put it on pause," she says. "We didn't cancel the expansion plans entirely."

Bowles says the expansion resumed once her company had dealt with some up-front costs to come into compliance with the net neutrality order. The pending demise of Title II had nothing to do with it. In fact, the expansion plans were resumed before the election.

Other ISPs said they haven't thought twice about continuing to expand. Rucker, at Monkeybrains, says his company has been growing 25 percent each quarter—in subscribers, profit, and employees—for the past five years, before and after net neutrality. "We're not reluctant to grow and have been building as fast as we can," he says.

Peggy Dolgenos, the co-founder and co-CEO of an ISP named Cruzio that's located in Santa Cruz, California, said her company has been rapidly improving its equipment. "We've been upgrading our infrastructure as fast as we can," she says. Her company currently has 35 employees and serves about 9,000 customers. "We've been investing like crazy. We're about to invest in a really big local project to install fiber optic cable in our downtown." She hopes to start offering the new fiber service sometime this fall.

Many smaller ISPs said they saw net neutrality as an advantage for their business, too. "If you're looking at what companies will get paid by big providers like Netflix, it's not smaller ISPs, it's large ISPs who already have practically a monopoly position," Dolgenos says. "They'll just cement their position, and it'll just crush competition."

Dane Jasper, CEO of Sonic, says he's concerned that larger internet providers will use paid traffic agreements and privacy-invasive ad-tracking policies to force smaller providers out of the market. Using that added revenue, he says, "it could be a dominant market player could sell to that subscriber for $5 to $10 a month less because they have these behind-the-scenes revenue sources that fall to them as a result of the overturn of the privacy protections and the re-categorization of Title II for broadband internet access."

Even Bowles, who says she disagrees with the Title II classification, says there are benefits. One of those is looser deployment rules around attaching telecom equipment to utility poles. "It allows you to go under the trees and makes it a lot easier," she says.

The FCC is now nearly halfway through the public comment period on its proposal to reverse net neutrality. By most indications, it looks like the commission intends to move ahead with the proposal regardless of the feedback it receives, allaying concerns about possible burdens on small businesses—but opening these smaller ISPs up to more threats from Comcast and the like as well. This is a big part of why just over 40 small ISPs wrote their own letter to the FCC last month requesting that net neutrality stay in place.

Dolgenos, of Cruzio, says she fears the FCC's deregulatory tendencies will push the ISP industry even closer to monopoly or duopoly. If more small providers are forced out, she says, the big ISPs will try to make more money off their existing customer base instead of continuing to expand. "How are we going to service rural or semi-rural?" Dolgenos asks. "There's no reason to do it if you have to put a line a mile up a road to reach four houses. It's just not going to happen."

> "While the free market always supports innovation and consumers' choices, government control has only led to corruption and inefficiency in all entities it controls."

We Don't Need Net Neutrality to Protect the Internet

Drew Armstrong

In the following viewpoint, Drew Armstrong argues that the rules passed by the FCC were unnecessary, because there have already been multiple internet protection regulations passed over the past twenty years by the Federal Trade Commission (FTC), which argued that the FCC's rules were unnecessary and would weaken consumer protections. Using the comparison of the old Bell Telephone Company monopoly, Armstrong points out that the development and growth of the internet as seen today would not have happened without the same deregulation and consumer protections passed by the FTC. Armstrong is a freelance political journalist based in Orange County, California.

As you read, consider the following questions:

1. What was one of the major, privately funded contributors to the Open Internet Order?
2. Is the point of net neutrality to eliminate telephone and cable companies and place control of those services and the internet in the hands of the federal government?
3. How could running the internet as a public utility inhibit or threaten its long-term usability?

The fight over the privacy rules passed by the Federal Communications Commission (FCC) is the latest brawl between advocates of a free and largely unregulated Internet and the "net neutrality" activist ideologues who see the Internet as something that should be nationalized and publicly owned and regulated.

In March, Congress voted 215–205 to eliminate the Internet privacy rules passed by the FCC under former chairman Tom Wheeler. The Senate had already voted the same way. President Trump signed the legislation into law in April [2017]. The vote in Congress was predictably condemned by ideologues opining in the *Washington Post*, CNN, and other news outlets on how the vote entirely destroys our privacy rights on the Internet. But repealing the draconian FCC privacy rules—before they were set to take effect later this year—will not put our privacy rights in any danger at all. There are more than enough federal and state protections in place.

We're Fine Without It, Thanks

Internet privacy has been protected quite well for almost 20 years by rules from the Federal Trade Commission (FTC). When the FCC enacted the new privacy rules, the FTC opposed them as unnecessary. Surely when the FTC says new rules would hurt consumers and weaken consumer protections, those rules should be seriously questioned. Without the FCC privacy rules, the FTC remains active in protecting consumer privacy on the Internet.

The privacy and net neutrality rules passed in the FCC in 2015 were part of the larger effort under the Obama Administration to regulate the Internet as if it were a public utility, much like the old "Ma Bell" phone monopoly. Ironically, the very development and growth of the Internet would not have been possible were it not for the deregulation and breaking up of the old phone monopoly.

Current FCC Chairman Ajit Pai pointed out that the elimination of the FCC Internet regulations will not harm consumers, or the public interest, because they were never needed. Justification for the regulations were "phantoms that were conjured up by people who wanted the FCC for political reasons to overregulate the Internet," he told Nick Gillespie of *Reason*. "We were not living in a digital dystopia in the years leading up to 2015." Pai also pointed out how Google and Facebook have succeeded in an Internet free of government micromanagement, where content providers and others are free to innovate and offer consumers the services and content they demand.

The "Open Internet Order" (OIO) regulating the Internet, passed by the FCC in 2015, would have moved the Internet in the direction favored by net neutrality ideologues. In the text of the OIO, the George Soros–funded net neutrality group Free Press was mentioned 46 times—it's almost as if Free Press had written the regulations for the FCC. The OIO sees the Internet as something that should be nationalized by the government to be run like a public utility.

Advocates of this vision, including leaders of Free Press, have made it clear what they want. Robert McChesney, one of the founders of Free Press, stated,

> What we want to have in the US and in every society is an Internet that is not private property, but a public utility. We want an Internet where you don't have to have a password and that you don't pay a penny to use. It is your right to use the Internet.

The goal they are calling "net neutrality" is to have the federal government, and governments around the world, in control of the Internet. McChesney stated further,

> At the moment, the battle over network neutrality is not to completely eliminate the telephone and cable companies. We are not at that point yet. But the ultimate goal is to get rid of the media capitalists in the phone and cable companies and to divest them from control.

Government control of the Internet raises many questions about consumer and privacy protection. When the Office of Personnel Management held the personal data of 21.5 million people, it was an easy target for hackers seeking access. The list of government agencies compromised by hackers continues to grow. Imagine if everyone's personal information, including emails, browser history, and the data stored on "cookies" on computers was stored in one giant government entity that runs the Internet.

Public Utilities Are Not Private

The FCC agenda that voted for those regulations in 2015 is less about privacy and consumer protection than it is about government control of the Internet. In receiving court approval of the privacy rules, the FCC reclassified broadband Internet access as a public utility.

The rapid advance of technology lets the Internet evolve continually, and this innovation is threatened if the Internet is to be regulated or run like a public utility. Public utilities do not compete against other entities, and are regulated as monopolies. But the Internet is not structured that way: most consumers have a choice in what Internet service they have. In 20 years, Internet providers invested more than $1.5 trillion in the development of the Internet in the US. Most homes in the US have access to broadband Internet at lower rates than consumers pay in Europe, where the service is price-regulated.

Public utilities do not innovate, nor do they seek to better their service for consumers. Those who remember the old "Ma Bell" phone monopoly know this: consumers rented phones from "the phone company" at high rates, and although getting them fixed was included in the cost of the service, consumers often waited days before a technician showed up.

There are two clear paths the Internet might take, depending on which side wins this battle over having a truly free, private Internet or one controlled by the government as a public utility. While the free market always supports innovation and consumers' choices, government control has only led to corruption and inefficiency in all entities it controls.

Supporters have communicated exactly what they want. There can be no confusion about what the net neutrality agenda is all about: supporters of net neutrality demonize Internet service providers in their populist arguments for government control. But if they win their dream, consumers will be the real losers in this battle over Internet control.

> *"This new blocking trend has been triggered in a number of countries as a result of increased piracy and intellectual property infringements on the Internet."*

Online Content Regulation Has Become a Focus of Governments Around the World

Yaman Akdeniz

In the following viewpoint, Yaman Akdeniz presents a study commissioned by the Organization for Security and Co-operation in Europe (OSCE) concerning freedom of media. This research is the first of its kind by the OSCE regarding internet content regulation in OSCE-participating nations. The study comments on the difficulties nations face in governing the internet, because it has become borderless with the advent of companies like YouTube, Facebook, and Twitter, which are used by consumers from all over the world. The study comes to twelve conclusions regarding how OSCE-participating nations should respect the principles of net neutrality and how to attempt to govern an international concept. Akdeniz is a professor at the Istanbul Bilgi University in Turkey.

"Freedom of Expression on the Internet, A Study of Legal Provisions and Practices Related to Freedom of Expression, the Free Flow of Information and Media Pluralism on the Internet in OSCE Participating States," by Yaman Akdeniz, OSCE Representative on Freedom of the Media, 2012. Reprinted by Permission.

As you read, consider the following questions:

1. What are the issues that may arise in countries that have internet "kill switch" plans?
2. How can a country attempt to manage the internet if the internet is and has become a global form of media?
3. Are the viewpoint's recommendations feasible on both a national and international level?

Whenever new communications and media platforms have been introduced, their innovation and application was met with scepticism, fear or outright banning by the ruling parties and authorities who feared the unknown medium, and its capacity to oust them from power. Therefore, new (mass) media historically face suspicion, and are liable to excessive regulation as they spark fear of potential detrimental effects on society, security and political power structures. This has proven true in the publication and transmission of certain types of content from the printing press through the advent of radio, television and satellite transmissions, as well as other forms of communication systems. During the 1990s, as attention turned to the Internet and as access to this borderless new communications platform increased, the widespread availability of various content, including sexually explicit content and other types of content deemed to be harmful for children, stirred up a "moral panic" shared by many states and governments and certain civil-society representatives and concerned citizens.

Prior to the 1990s, information and content was predominantly within the strict boundaries and control of individual states, whether through paper-based publications, audio-visual transmissions limited to a particular area or even through public demonstrations and debates. Much of the media content made available and the discussions it triggered remained confined within territorially defined areas. Today, however, information and content, with its digital transmission and widespread availability through the Internet, do not necessarily respect national rules or territorial boundaries.

This dissolution of the "sovereignty" of content control, coupled with the globalization of information, comes along with an increased multilingualism observable in many countries. The increasing popularity of user-driven interactive Web 2.0 applications and services such as YouTube, Facebook and Twitter seem to eliminate virtual Internet borders even further by creating a seamless global public sphere. This, inevitably complicates state-level efforts to find an appropriate balance between the universal right to freedom of opinion and expression, which includes the right to receive and impart information, and the prohibition on certain types of content deemed illegal by nation-state authorities or intergovernmental organizations. With the widespread availability of the Internet and increasing number of users, online content regulation became an important focus of governments and supranational bodies across the globe.

Today, many OSCE participating States feel the need to react to the development of the Internet as a major media and communication platform. Governments think that it is, on the one hand, the infrastructure that requires protective measures and, on the other hand, content made available that necessitates regulation. The past few years have shown that more people access the Internet, more content is made available online and more states feel obliged to regulate online content. A number of countries across the OSCE region have introduced new legal provisions in response to the availability and dissemination of certain types of (illegal or unwanted) content. Governments are particularly concerned about the availability of terrorist propaganda, racist content, hate speech, sexually explicit content, including child pornography, as well as state secrets and content critical to certain governments or business practices. However, the governance of illegal as well as harmful (which falls short of illegal) Internet content may differ from one country to another and variations are evident within the OSCE participating States. "Harm criteria" remain distinct within different jurisdictions with individual states deciding what is legal and illegal based upon different cultural, moral, religious and historical differences and constitutional values.

Typically, the stance taken by many states is that what is illegal and punishable in an offline form must at least be treated equally online. There are, however, several features of the Internet which fundamentally affect approaches to its governance and while rules and boundaries still exist, enforcement of existing laws, rules and regulations to digital content becomes evidently complex and problematic. Despite the introduction of new laws or amendments to existing laws criminalizing publication or distribution of certain types of content, in almost all instances extraterritoriality remains a major problem when content hosted or distributed from outside the jurisdiction is deemed illegal in another. Therefore, the question of jurisdiction over content adds to the challenges faced by the governments and regulators. Which country's laws should apply for content providers or for Web 2.0 based platform providers? Should the providers be liable in the country where the content has been uploaded, viewed, or downloaded or where the server is placed or where the responsible providers reside? Many of these questions remain unanswered. Some countries fear the Internet could undermine their judicial sovereignty; others embrace the Internet and praise its global nature. However, the Internet certainly has created challenges for governments and these challenges are particularly visible when analyzing measures aimed at regulating online content.

Based on the limited effectiveness of state laws and lack of harmonization at international level (despite some efforts at regional level that will be addressed in this study) a number of states, including some in the OSCE region, introduced policies to block access to Internet content, websites deemed illegal and Web 2.0 based social media platforms which are outside their jurisdiction. The new trend in Internet regulation seems to entail blocking access to content if state authorities are not in a position to reach the perpetrators for prosecution or if their request for removal or take down of such content is rejected or ignored by foreign law enforcement authorities or hosting and content providers.

Furthermore, in certain countries, governments went further and developed measures which could restrict users' access to the Internet. This new blocking trend has been triggered in a number of countries as a result of increased piracy and intellectual property infringements on the Internet. These developments, as well as new policy trends in Internet content regulation, are detailed in this study.

While the intention of states to combat illegal activity over the Internet and to protect their citizens from harmful content is legitimate, there are also significant legal and policy developments which directly or indirectly and sometimes have an unintended negative impact on freedom of expression and the free flow of information. Recent laws and certain legal measures currently under development have provoked much controversy over the past few years.

Concerned with such developments, the OSCE Representative on Freedom of the Media commissioned a report to assess whether and how access to and content on the Internet are regulated across the OSCE region by examining existing laws and practices related to freedom of expression, the free flow of information and media pluralism. This first OSCE-wide content regulation study also provides a comprehensive overview of existing international legal provisions and standards relating to media freedom and freedom of expression on the Internet. The study aims to assess whether and how these provisions are incorporated into national legislation by the OSCE participating States.

The report also assesses the compliance of applicable national Internet legislation and practices with existing OSCE media freedom commitments, Article 19 of the Universal Declaration of Human Rights, Article 19 of the International Covenant on Civil and Political Rights, Article 10 of the European Convention on Human Rights (where applicable) as well as the case law of the European Court of Human Rights.

[…]

The analysis of the data and information provided by the participating States on Internet content regulation leads to the following conclusions and recommendations:

The Open and Global Nature of the Internet Should Be Ensured

Participating States need to take action to ensure that the Internet remains as an open and public forum for freedom of opinion and expression, as guaranteed by OSCE commitments, enshrined in the Universal Declaration of Human Rights, the International Covenant on Civil and Political Rights, and the European Convention on Human Rights. OSCE participating States should keep in mind the borderless nature of the Internet when developing online content regulation policies. The preservation of the global nature of the Internet requires participating States to consider regional and alternative approaches to online content regulation.

Access to the Internet Should Be Regarded as a Human Right and Recognized as Implicit to the Right to Free Expression and Free Information

Access to the Internet remains the most important prerequisite to be part of and take part in the Information Society. Access to the Internet is one of the basic prerequisites to the right to freedom of expression and the right to impart and receive information regardless of frontiers. As such, access to the Internet should be recognized as a fundamental human right.

The Right to Freedom of Expression Is Universal —Also in Regard to the Medium and Technology

The right to freedom of expression and freedom of the media were not designed to fit a particular medium, technology or platform. Freedom of expression applies to all means of communications, including the Internet. Restrictions to this right are only acceptable if in compliance with international norms and standards. Any restriction should be weighed against the public interest.

New Technologies Require New Approaches

Typically, the stance taken by the participating States is that what is illegal and punishable in an offline form must at least be treated equally online. There are, however, several features of the Internet which fundamentally affect approaches to its governance. While rules and boundaries still exist, enforcement of existing laws, rules and regulations to digital content becomes evidently complex, problematic and at times impossible to enforce on the Internet. Participating States should develop alternative approaches adapted to the specific nature of the Internet. Participating States should also place more emphasis on Internet and media literacy projects for vulnerable groups, particularly children.

Network Neutrality Should Be Respected

Legal or technical measures regarding end-users' access to or use of services and applications through the Internet should respect the fundamental rights and freedoms guaranteed by international human rights principles, especially freedom of expression and the free flow of information. Online information and traffic should be treated equally regardless of the device, content, author, origin or destination. Service providers should make their information management practices of online data transparent and accessible.

Furthermore, information society service provision should not be subject to governmental barriers and strict licensing regimes.

Internet "Kill Switch" Plans Should Be Avoided

Existent legal provisions allow several participating States to completely suspend all Internet communication and "switch off" Internet access for whole populations or segments of the public during times of war, states of emergency and in cases of imminent threat to national security. Reaffirming the importance of fully respecting the right to freedom of opinion and expression, the participating States should refrain from developing, introducing and applying "Internet kill switch" plans as they are incompatible with the fundamental right to information.

OSCE Participating States Should Avoid Vague Legal Terminology in Speech-Based Restrictions

Definitional problems and inconsistencies exist with regard to certain speech-based restrictions. Clarifications are needed to define what amounts to "extremism," "terrorist propaganda," "harmful" and "racist content" and "hate speech." Legal provisions are often vague and open to wide or subjective interpretation. Any restriction must meet the strict criteria under international and regional human rights law. The necessity for restricting the right to speak and receive information must be convincingly established to be compatible with international human rights standards.

OSCE Participating States Should Refrain from Mandatory Blocking of Content or Websites

Given the limited effectiveness of national laws and the lack of harmonization at the international level to prosecute criminal online content, a number of OSCE participating States started to block access to online content deemed illegal and Web 2.0 based social media platforms outside of their jurisdiction. Since blocking mechanisms are not immune from significant deficiencies, they may result in the blocking of access to legitimate sites and content. Further, blocking is an extreme measure and has a very strong impact on freedom of expression and the free flow of information. Participating States should therefore refrain from using blocking as a permanent solution or as a means of punishment. Indefinite blocking of access to websites and Internet content could result to "prior restraint" and by suspending access to websites indefinitely states can largely overstep the narrow margin of appreciation afforded to them by international norms and standards.

Blocking of online content can only be justified if in accordance with these standards and done pursuant to court order and where absolutely necessary. Blocking criteria should always be made public and provide for legal redress.

Voluntary Blocking and Content Removal Arrangements Should Be Transparent and Open to Appeal

Voluntary blocking measures and agreements exist in a number of participating States. However, private hotlines do not always have legal authority to require ISPs to block access to websites or to require removal of content. Any blocking system based exclusively on self-regulation or voluntary agreements between state actors and private actors have to be conceived in a way as not to interfere with fundamental rights. Furthermore, blocking criteria of hotlines and private actors are not always transparent or open to appeal. Any blocking or removal system based on self-regulation and voluntary agreements should be transparent, compatible with international norms and standards and provide for redress mechanisms and judicial remedies.

Filtering Should Only Be Encouraged as an End-User Voluntary Measure

OSCE participating States should encourage the use of end-user filtering software on individual home computers and in schools if their use is deemed necessary. However, the deployment of state-level upstream filtering systems, as well as government-mandated filtering systems, should be avoided. If the use of filters is encouraged by the states, users should be made aware of the potential limitations of filtering software as there are serious questions about the reliability of such tools as stand-alone solutions for child protection.

"Three-Strikes" Measures to Protect Copyright Are Incompatible with the Right to Information

The development of so-called "three-strikes" legal measures to combat Internet piracy in a number of participating States is worrisome. While countries have a legitimate interest to combat piracy, restricting or cutting off users' access to the Internet is a disproportionate response which is incompatible with OSCE commitments on the freedom to seek, receive and impart information, a right which in fact should be strengthened by the Internet. Participating States should refrain from developing or adopting legal measures which could result [in] restricting citizens' access to the Internet. A discussion on whether or not current international standards on intellectual property protection are suited for our information society might be necessary.

Reliable Information on Applicable Legislation and Blocking Statistics Needs to Be Made Available

Despite the high responsiveness of the participating States to take part in the survey, many governments expressed major difficulties in collecting the requested data because reliable or recorded information was not available or different governmental institutions and ministries are responsible for the different aspects of the Internet. Almost no participating State had an institutional focal point on Internet matters to rely on. It is recommended that participating States put mechanisms in place that allow for the maintenance of reliable information on Internet content regulation and statistical data pertaining to questions on blocking statistics and prosecutions for speech-related offenses committed on the Internet. These statistics and information should be made available to the public.

Participating States should also increase their efforts to better co-ordinate and share information on Internet content regulation.

Periodical and Internet Sources Bibliography

The following articles have been selected to supplement the diverse views presented in this chapter.

Tali Arbel, "FCC Chief Defends Internet Plans by Attacking Twitter," Associated Press, November 28, 2017. https://www.mercurynews .com/2017/11/28/fcc-chief-defends-internet-plans-by-attacking -twitter/

Fran Berkman and Andrew Couts, "Title II Is the Key to Net Neutrality—So What Is It?," *Daily Dot*, May 20, 2014. https:// www.dailydot.com/layer8/what-is-title-ii-net-neutrality-fcc/.

Michelle Castillo and Todd Haselton, "The FCC Has Reversed a 2015 Rule That Could Change How You Access and Pay for Internet Service," CNBC, December 14, 2017. https://www.cnbc.com /2017/12/14/fcc-reverses-open-internet-order-governing-net -neutrality.html.

Kenneth Corbin, "House Moves to Defund FCC Net Neutrality Rules," InternetNews.com, February 18, 2011. http://www .internetnews.com/government/article.php/3925561 /HouseMoves-to-Defund-FCC-Net-Neutrality-Rules.htm.

Michael Hiltzik, "FCC Chairman Pai Defends His Attack on Net Neutrality by Substituting Ideology for History," *Los Angeles Times*, November 29, 2017. http://beta.latimes.com/business /hiltzik/la-fi-hiltzik-pai-speech-20171129-story.html.

Timothy B. Lee, "Network Neutrality, Explained," Vox, May 21, 2015. https://www.vox.com/cards/network-neutrality/what-is-the -open-internet-order.

Cherlynn Low, "What You Need to Know About Net Neutrality (Before It Gets Taken Away)," *Engadget* (blog), December 1, 2017. https://www.engadget.com/2017/12/01/net-neutrality-faq-title-i -title-ii-2017/.

Terrell McSweeny and John Sallet, "Kill the Open Internet, and Wave Goodbye to Consumer Choice," *Wired*, July 3, 2017. https://www .wired.com/story/kill-the-open-internet-and-wave-goodbye-to -consumer-choice/.

Bruce M. Owen, "Antecedents to Net Neutrality," *Regulation* 30, no. 3 (2007). https://papers.ssrn.com/sol3/papers.cfm?abstract _id=1025966.

Oyez, "*Verizon Communications, Inc. v. Law Offices of Curtis V. Trinco, LLP*," October 14, 2003. www.oyez.org/cases/2003/02-682.

Brett Samuels, "FCC Chief: Critics of Net Neutrality Rollback Overstate Fears," *Hill* (Washington, DC), November 22, 2017. http://thehill.com/policy/technology/361521-pai-on-net -neutrality-we-need-more-investment-not-micromanaging.

Ben Thompson, "Pro-Neutrality, Anti-Title II," Stratechery, November 28, 2017. https://stratechery.com/2017/pro-neutrality -anti-title-ii/.

Kate Tummarello, "FCC Chief: Critics 'Flat Out Wrong,'" *Hill* (Washington, DC), April 24, 2014. http://thehill.com/policy /technology/204247-fcc-chief-defends-new-net-neutrality -proposal.

US House of Representatives and US Senate, "Communications Act of 1934," United States of America in Congress, 1934. https:// transition.fcc.gov/Reports/1934new.pdf.

Robert Winterton, "Net Neutrality v. Title II: Explained," Tech Policy Corner, May 15, 2017. https://techpolicycorner.org/net -neutrality-v-title-ii-explained-3ad8d576a50a.

CHAPTER 3

Will the Internet Become Segregated Without Net Neutrality?

Chapter Preface

What protects consumers of the internet if not strict net neutrality regulations? Or do consumers even need to be concerned in the first place? In the opening viewpoint of this chapter, Maureen K. Ohlhausen of the FTC points out not only that the FCC's 2015 regulations were heavy-handed and unnecessary but also that there is no reason for consumers to fear the censorship so often discussed within the argument of net neutrality, because there is not enough competition among broadband companies to warrant censorship.

But while there is no current indication that major ISPs are leaning in a direction that would lead to paid prioritization, throttling, and similar censorship, there is also no indication that these companies won't act in that manner in the future, especially as the battle over access to the internet continues. Finding a decision that will suit both the company and the consumer will be a difficult battle that many have compared to that of the civil rights movement of the 1960s. Similar to the efforts made toward racial equality, grassroots efforts were key in the US Court of Appeals decision to preserve the FCC's 2015 Open Internet Order—and it is likely that those efforts will continue to have a significant impact on the preservation of open access to the internet, no matter the political regime in power or the regulations passed by organizations like the FCC and FTC.

No matter the overall policy and whether its turned into law through congressional intervention, viewpoints in this chapter make it clear that it is important for ISPs to have clear and consistent company regulations regarding the services they offer and that these company policies must be transparent and easy to understand by the consumers using their products.

> *"Competition, facilitated through effective antitrust and consumer protection enforcement, is all the protection that ISP and edge provider markets need to operate effectively."*

We Should Take Competition in Broadband Seriously

Maureen K. Ohlhausen

In the following viewpoint, an excerpt from a report by the FTC, Maureen K. Ohlhausen argues that the net neutrality regulations passed by the FCC are unnecessary, due to the already existing provisions laid out by antitrust regulations. Ohlhausen contends that there is no reason for consumers to be concerned about this form of censorship or limited access, because there is not enough competition between ISPs due to the current lack of infrastructure, which is further limited by net neutrality rules. Ohlhausen is acting chair of the FTC.

"Antitrust over Net Neutrality: Why We Should Take Competition in Broadband Seriously," by Maureen K. Ohlhausen, Federal Trade Commission.

As you read, consider the following questions:

1. Why does the author have confidence in letting antitrust regulations protect the internet, rather than net neutrality?
2. According to Ohlhausen, what are some arguments in favor of ISPs prioritizing certain content?
3. What actions initially hindered the FCC's efforts to require net neutrality regulations?

Can competition, backed up by antitrust, guard the public interest online? The net neutrality movement does not think so. Its proponents make two erroneous claims. First, they say that antitrust will not stop Internet service providers (ISPs) from using anticompetitive practices to exclude rival content. Second, they contend that market forces do not protect nonmonetary values like Internet openness, democratic participation, viewpoint diversity, and free speech. Net neutrality advocates worry that ISPs may undermine those goals, as well as competition, by disfavoring some content running through their last-mile networks. Hence, the net neutrality crowd proclaims *ex ante* regulation is essential because antitrust is not up to the job. That conclusion is misplaced, but it has proven influential. In its 2015 Open Internet Order, the Federal Communications Commission (FCC) reclassified broadband ISPs as "common carriers" under Title II of the 1934 Communications Act.[1] Using the regulatory power thus unlocked, the FCC prohibited throttling, blocking, and paid prioritization.[2] In doing so, it rejected competitive market forces and antitrust as sufficient alternatives to regulation. Specifically, the FCC did "not find existing laws sufficient to adequately protect consumers' access to the open Internet" and rejected the "suggest[ion] that existing antitrust laws would address discriminatory conduct of an anticompetitive nature."[3] Remarkably, the agency saw no need to evaluate ISPs' market power before rejecting the curative powers of competition. In its view, "threats to Internet-enabled innovation, growth, and competition do not depend on broadband providers having market power with respect to their end users."[4] Hence, the FCC determined that it "need not consider whether market concentration gives broadband providers the ability to raise prices."[5] Cementing its rejection of markets, the agency concluded that, "even if the mobile market were sufficiently competitive, competition alone is not sufficient to deter mobile providers from taking actions that would limit Internet openness."[6]

Net neutrality regulation reflects a lack of confidence in market forces that I do not share. Antitrust can protect the competitive sphere in which edge providers and ISPs operate. And it can also promote nonpecuniary values like openness and free speech. That last claim may strike some readers as counter-intuitive, but recall that antitrust serves a prophylactic function. It guards the competitive process, which in turn leads firms to satisfy consumers' revealed preferences. Antitrust does not dictate market outcomes, in the way that *ex ante* regulation like the 2015 Open Internet Order does. Rather, it trusts that markets—free of artificial restraints on trade and exclusionary practices—tend toward efficiency in meeting consumers' demand, including their demand for "nonpecuniary" values.[7] The FCC's move to ban all paid prioritization, among other practices, takes the form of a *per se* rule that antitrust would never countenance for such vertical restraints.

The US Supreme Court has explained that the "heart of our national economic policy has been faith in the value of competition."[8] This article explains that such faith remains justified online. Competition, facilitated through effective antitrust and consumer protection enforcement, is all the protection that ISP and edge provider markets need to operate effectively.[9] To the extent that ISP consumers value norms like openness and civic participation, it is not true that ISPs, free of net neutrality rules, would disregard them. To the contrary, competitive markets respond to consumer demand.[10] If ISP subscribers would abhor any deviation from equal treatment of data, then market outcomes should serve the nonmonetary goals that net neutrality advocates champion. Certainly, the paucity of real life examples of net neutrality violations is telling. But sometimes prioritized treatment may be of tremendous value to consumers. And that means that a liberalized, competitive market may sometimes produce outcomes in tension with net neutrality advocates' ideological vision. The 2015 Open Internet Order prevents that outcome, effectively displacing consumer demand with a political viewpoint.

Consider that it may be efficient for some ISPs to market plans that prioritize certain content. When congestion occurs, the traditional Internet norm is first in, first out. But not all content is equally valuable to all end users or equally susceptible to latency. Net neutrality is blind to content, however, requiring the same treatment of acutely important content as the banal and offensive. For instance, ISPs must treat telemedicine and pornography the same. Yet some ISP subscribers are avid gamers, who would pay a premium for guaranteed, lightning-fast connections. And others have an affinity for HD movies. There are distinctions even within those groups. In normal markets, firms would respond to varied tastes by providing services tailored to consumer demand.

But the FCC's no-discrimination rule freezes the market at the *status quo*. Its ban on paid prioritization, in particular, rejects a core premise on which all markets operate: price signals allocate scarce resources more efficiently than other systems. As the Supreme Court has long observed, "[p]rice is the 'central nervous system of the economy.'"[11] Net neutrality discards that system, condemning vertical restraints common to many competitive markets and, in the process, reveals a political disposition in some tension with the core tenets of the US capitalist, market system. The 2015 Open Internet Order crystallizes content-blind "best efforts" as the governing rule, regardless of shifts in consumer demand, network capacity, or content. That shortcoming illustrates a general problem with regulation: inflexibility to changing market conditions.

In short, net neutrality proponents underestimate the ability of market forces, combined with antitrust oversight, to shield consumers from harmful ISP content discrimination. As the Supreme Court has explained, the "assumption that competition is the best method of allocating resources in a free market recognizes that all elements of a bargain—quality, service, safety, and durability— and not just the immediate cost, are favorably affected by the free opportunity to select among alternative offers."[12] Those dynamics apply equally to ISP markets as they do to other sectors of the economy. This article makes the case for a market-based solution to ISP conduct.

Part I of this article contextualizes the 2015 Open Internet Order in light of previous efforts by the FCC to impose net neutrality rules. It explains that the FCC saw market based competition and antitrust enforcement as inadequate substitutes for *ex ante* regulation. The agency held that view, despite little evidence of net neutrality violations to date, and without analyzing ISPs' market power.

I. The FCC'S Net Neutrality Rules

A. Prologue: The Courts First Rebuff the FCC's Net Neutrality Efforts

The FCC has long sought to address concerns about potential ISP misconduct. In 2005, the FCC adopted a policy statement with four principles, which collectively expressed the agency's net neutrality position.[13] Although it did not adopt rules, the agency stated that, subject to reasonable network management:

(1) consumers are entitled to access the lawful Internet content of their choice; (2) consumers are entitled to run applications and services of their choice, subject to the needs of law enforcement; (3) consumers are entitled to connect their choice of legal devices that do not harm the network; and (4) consumers are entitled to competition among network providers, application and service providers, and content providers.[14]

The first—and to date one of the few evidenced net neutrality ISP violations—occurred the same year. Madison River Communication reportedly blocked ports for Voice over Internet

LIKELY SCENARIOS

The Electronic Frontier Foundation (EFF) urged the FCC to keep in place net neutrality rules, which are essential to prevent cable companies like Comcast and Verizon from controlling, censoring, and discriminating against their subscribers' favorite Internet content.

EFF came out strongly in opposition to the FCC's plan to reverse the agency's 2015 open Internet rules, which were designed to guarantee that service providers treat everyone's content equally. The reversal would send a clear signal that those providers can engage in data discrimination, such as blocking websites, slowing down Internet speeds for certain content and charging subscribers fees to access movies, social media, and other entertainment content over "fast lanes." Given the lack of competition, the potential for abuse is very real.

EFF's comments join those of many other user advocates, leading computer engineers, entrepreneurs, faith communities, libraries, educators, tech giants, and start-ups that are fighting for a free and open Internet … those players gave the Internet a taste of what a world without net neutrality would look like by temporarily blocking and throttling their content. Such scenarios aren't merely possible—they are likely, EFF said in its comments. Internet service providers (ISPs) have already demonstrated that they are willing to discriminate against competitors and block content for their own benefit, while harming the Internet experience of users.

"ISPs have incentives to shape Internet traffic and the FCC knows full well of instances where consumers have been harmed. AT&T blocked data sent by Apple's FaceTime software, Comcast has interfered with Internet traffic generated by certain applications, and ISPs have rerouted users' web searches to websites they didn't request or expect," said EFF Senior Staff Attorney Mitch Stoltz. "These are just some examples of ISPs controlling our Internet experience. Users pay them to connect to the Internet, not decide for them what they can see and do there."

Nearly 200 computer scientists, network engineers, and Internet professionals also submitted comments today highlighting deep flaws in the FCC's technical description of how the Internet works. The FCC is attempting to pass off its incorrect technical analysis to justify its plan to reclassify ISPs so they are not subject to net neutrality rules. The engineers' submission sets the record straight about how the Internet works and how rolling back net neutrality would have disastrous effects on Internet innovation.

"EFF to FCC: Tossing Net Neutrality Protections Will Set ISPs Free to Throttle, Block, and Censor the Internet for Users," Electronic Frontier Foundation, July 17, 2017.

Protocol (VoIP) on Madison's network. Shortly after receiving a complaint from Vonage, the FCC entered into a consent decree with Madison River, which agreed to pay $15,000 and not to prevent its customers from using VoIP applications.[15]

Questions about the FCC's regulatory authority hobbled the agency's subsequent efforts to require net neutrality. The FCC's first net neutrality related action against an ISP post-Madison River occurred in 2008, after Comcast allegedly interfered with its subscribers' peer-to-peer networking applications. Comcast maintained that it was simply managing its limited network capacity. The FCC issued a 2008 order, ruling that Comcast had "'significantly impeded consumers' ability to access the content and use the applications of their choice" and had alternative means to manage its network traffic without resorting to non-neutral treatment of content.[16] The agency's efforts to police the ISP's network-management practices, however, failed under scrutiny from the DC Circuit.[17] The court held that the FCC failed to identify statutory authority for its order.[18] Specifically, because the FCC had long classified ISPs as information services under Title I,[19] it could not rely on its ancillary authority under Section 4(i) of the 1934 Communications Act to justify its 2008 order. In particular, there was no link between the 2008 order and "a statutory delegation of regulatory authority."[20] Further, although Section 706(a) arguably delegated regulatory authority to the FCC, the court held that the agency could not rely on that provision in light of a then-existing FCC order."[21]

The FCC tried again to implement net neutrality rules two years later in its 2010 Open Internet Order.[22] Revisiting its interpretation of Section 706(a), the agency read the provision as allowing it to take action to develop broadband infrastructure. On that basis, the FCC adopted rules on transparency, blocking, and unreasonable discrimination.[23] Under the 2010 Order, fixed (as opposed to mobile) broadband providers could not block lawful content, applications, services, or non-harmful devices. Nor could they unreasonably discriminate in transmitting lawful network traffic.[24] The FCC explained, "As a general matter, it is unlikely that pay for priority would satisfy the 'no unreasonable discrimination' standard."[25] The rules were slightly looser for mobile ISPs: they could not block lawful content or applications that compete with their voice or voice-telephone services. All ISPs had to disclose their network management practices. The agency subjected fixed and wireless ISPs to some different rules—in particular, the FCC did not apply anti-discrimination rules to mobile ISPs—because in the FCC's view the mobile space was more competitive than the fixed ISP market.[26]

The 2010 Open Internet Order, however, failed judicial review in *Verizon* in 2014.[27] The DC Circuit accepted the FCC's interpretation of Section 706 as granting it regulatory authority. Nevertheless, the court struck down the 2010 Order because it essentially regulated fixed broadband ISPs as common carriers. The heart of the FCC's net neutrality order—the anti-discrimination and anti-blocking rules—treated ISPs as telecommunications services, even though the FCC had classified ISPs as information services under Title I. The DC Circuit thus vacated the FCC's anti-discrimination and anti-blocking rules.[28]

The 2014 ruling in *Verizon* created a quandary for the FCC and reignited the public debate over net neutrality regulation. Although the FCC had lost two rulings in four years in trying to enforce anti-discrimination rules against broadband ISPs, it was not all bad news for the agency. The *Verizon* court accepted Section 706 as a jurisdictional basis for regulating fixed and mobile broadband. To some net neutrality advocates, the path forward after *Verizon* was obvious: follow the court's prescribed pathway by using Section 706 authority to justify net neutrality regulation. For other advocates, the better path was for the FCC to reclassify broadband ISPs as telecommunications services and regulate them as common carriers under Title II.

ISPs, however, viewed the latter outcome as a distressing scenario. Title II means utility-style regulation by which the government has the authority (and in some cases the duty) to set rates, impose equal treatment obligations, require unbundling of network elements, and otherwise deprive private firms of the ability to operate as they would in a free market. The typical justification for common carrier regulation—natural monopoly—is absent from the broadband ISP market.[29] Further, enacted in 1934 to regulate telephone monopolies, Title II imposes some duties that are archaic and ill-suited to the realities of the modern Internet. Thus, reclassifying broadband ISPs under Title II was an extreme approach.

Shortly after *Verizon*, the FCC sparked a furor in some quarters when it proposed broadband ISP rules that would prohibit blocking and discriminating against lawful content, but would allow edge providers to pay for fast-lane access to end users if the ISP made the same opportunities available to other content providers on "commercially reasonable" terms.[30] Proponents of net neutrality denounced the proposal, arguing that favoring content providers who "pay to play" is improper discrimination. Leading a group of nearly 150 Silicon Valley firms, Google and Netflix wrote to the FCC, calling on the agency to ban paid prioritization and to reclassify broadband ISPs under Title II.[31] Most dramatically, after comedian John Oliver went on a pro net neutrality rant in June 2014 and called on viewers to tell the FCC their views, the FCC's comments website crashed after it received over 45,000 comments.[32] In November of that year, President Obama pressed the FCC to reclassify ISPs, arguing that "[c]able companies . . . can't let any company pay for priority over its competitors."[33] The FCC reversed course, adopting the Open Internet Order in February 2015.[34] In doing so, it reclassified broadband ISPs under Title II.[35]

Endnotes

1. *Protecting and Promoting the Open Internet*, GN. Dkt. No. 14-28, Report & Order on Remand, Declaratory Ruling, 30 FCC Rcd. 5601, 5743, para. 331 (2015) [hereinafter 2015 Open Internet Order].

2. Id. at 5607, paras. 15–18; *U.S. Telecomm. Ass'n v. FCC*, 825 F.3d 674, 733, (D.C. Cir. 2016) (Williams, J., concurring in part and dissenting in part).

3. 2015 Open Internet Order, supra note 1, at 5645, para. 104 n.237.

4. Id. at 5633, para. 84.

5. Id.

6. Id. at 5665, para. 148.

7. This article uses the terms "nonpecuniary" and "nonmonetary" values in the context of the net neutrality debate to refer to free speech, civic participation, openness, and related goals that justify rules against blocking, throttling, and paid participation. In economic terms, however, it does not make sense to refer to qualities that consumers value—and hence would pay for—as "nonpecuniary" and "nonmonetary." This point feeds into a central argument of this article. ISP markets, overseen by active antitrust enforcement, would produce broadband access plans that satisfy consumer demand. Hence, it is erroneous to reject an antitrust market solution to net neutrality issues.

8. *Standard Oil Co. v. FTC*, 340 U.S. 231, 249 (1951).

9. Consumer protection enforcement helps ensure ISPs provide the particular service attributes promised to consumers, whether it is speed, cost, or access to particular content.

10. This proposition is true of competitive markets across all industries. See, e.g., Christopher Sprigman, The 99¢ Question, 5 *J. ON TELECOMM. & HIGH TECH. L.* 87, 92 (2006) ("In a competitive market, we ordinarily would expect firms to respond to these different forms of demand."); Clayton P. Gillette & James E. Krier, Risk, Courts, and Agencies, 138 *U. PA. L. REV.* 1027, 1038 (1990).

11. *Nat'l Soc'y of Prof'l Eng'rs v. United States*, 435 U.S. 679, 692 (1978) (quoting *United States v. Socony-Vacuum Oil Co.*, 310 U.S. 150, 226 n.59 (1940)).

12. Id. at 695.

13. Appropriate Framework for Broadband Access to the Internet Over Wireline Facilities, CC Dkt. Nos. 02-33, 01-337, 95-20, 98-10, GN Dkt. No. 00-185, CS Dkt No. 05-52, Policy Statement, 20 FCC Rcd. 14,986, 14,988, para. 4 (2005).

14. Id.

15. Madison River Commc'ns, LLC, File No. EB-05-IH-110, Consent Decree, 20 FCC Rcd. 4296, 4297, paras. 4–5 (2005).

16. Formal Complaint of Free Press & Pub. Knowledge Against Comcast Corp. for Secretly Degrading Peer-to-Peer Applications, WC Dkt. No. 07-52, Memorandum Opinion & Order, 23 FCC Rcd. 13,028, 13,058, para. 51 (2008).

17. *Comcast Corp. v. FCC*, 600 F.3d 642 (D.C. Cir. 2010).

18. Id. at 661.

19. Starting in 2005 and until 2015, the FCC classified broadband ISPs as "information services" under Title I of the 1934 Communications Act, rather than as "telecommunications services" under Title II. Inquiry Concerning High-Speed Access to the Internet Over Cable and Other Facilities; Internet Over Cable Declaratory Ruling; Appropriate Regulatory Treatment for Broadband Access to the Internet Over Cable Facilities, GN Dckt. No. 00-185, Declaratory Ruling & Notice of Proposed Rulemaking, 17 FCC Rcd. 4798, 4824, para. 41 (2002); Appropriate Framework for Broadband Access to the Internet Over Wireline Facilities, CC Dkt. No. 02-33, Policy Statement, 20 FCC Rcd. 14,853, 14,862, para. 12 (2005); Appropriate Regulatory Treatment for Broadband Access to the Internet Over Wireless Networks, WT Dkt. No. 07-53, Declaratory Ruling, 22 FCC Rcd. 5901, 5901–02, para. 1 (2007); United Power Line Council's Petition for Declaratory Ruling Regarding the Classification of Broadband over Power Line Internet Access Service as an Information Service, WC Dkt. No. 06-10, Memorandum Opinion & Order, 21 FCC Rcd. 13,281, 13,281, para. 1 (2006). Title II imposes a host of regulatory duties, including charging "just and reasonable" rates and refraining from "unjust or unreasonable discrimination." 47 U.S.C. § 201(b), 202(a) (2012). Those provisions have no analogue under Title I. Indeed, later in 2005, the Supreme Court upheld the FCC's classification of a fixed broadband provider as an information service. *Nat'l Cable & Telcomm'cns Ass'n v. Brand X Internet Servs.*, 545 U.S. 967 (2005).

20. *Comcast*, 600 F.3d at 658.

21. Id. at 658–59 (citing Deployment of Wireline Servs. Offering Advanced Telecomm. Capability, CC Dkt. No. 98-147, Memorandum Opinion & Order, & Notice of Proposed Rulemaking, 13 FCC Rcd. 24,012, 24,044, para. 69 (1998)).

22. Preserving the Open Internet, GN Dkt. No. 09-191, Report & Order, 25 FCC Rcd. 17,905 (2010).

23. Id. at 17906, para. 1.

24. Id.

25. Id. at 17947, para. 76.

26. Id. at 17956–57, paras. 94–95.

27. *Verizon v. FCC*, 740 F.3d 623, 626 (D.C. Cir. 2014).

28. Id. at 628.

29. See, e.g., Daniel F. Spulber & Christopher S. Yoo, Rethinking Broadband Internet Access, 22 *HARV. J.L. & TECH.* 1, 2–3, 21–27 (2008).

30. Protecting and Promoting the Open Internet, WC Dkt. No. 14-28, Notice of Proposed Rulemaking, 29 FCC Rcd. 5561, 5583, para. 61 (2014).

31. See, e.g., Brian Fung, Google, Netflix Lead Nearly 150 Tech Companies in Protest of FCC Net Neutrality Plan, *WASH. POST* (May 7, 2014), http://wpo.st/MBt72 [https://perma.cc/HEN7-HAT8].

32. See Soraya Nadia McDonald, John Oliver's Net Neutrality Rant May Have Caused FCC Site Crash, *WASH. POST* (June 4, 2014), http://wpo.st/5Ct72 [https://perma .cc/G79U-K38S] ("[T]he FCC's commenting system had stopped working, thanks to more than 45,000 new comments on net neutrality likely sparked by Oliver.").

33. The White House, President Obama's Statement on Keeping the Internet Open and Free, YOUTUBE (Nov. 10, 2014), https://www.youtube.com/watch?v=uKcjQPVwfDk [https://perma.cc/3Q9N-YR8V].

> *"Despite being a simple idea, net neutrality has proven difficult to translate into US policy."*

Net Neutrality and Regulation Are a Tangled Web

Larry Downes

In the following viewpoint, Larry Downes argues that there is a solution that would satisfy both those who are for the net neutrality regulations and those who oppose such regulations. Downes points out that many of the net neutrality proponents like Google and Netflix are not in support of the public utility reclassification due to concerns about government regulation of the internet. Downes is a senior fellow with Accenture Research and a coauthor of Big Bang Disruption: Strategy in the Age of Devastating Innovation *and* Unleashing the Killer App *(Portfolio, 2014).*

As you read, consider the following questions:

1. Which major company CEO acknowledged that net neutrality principles will be enforced with or without the FCC rules?
2. What caused the FCC to turn the open internet principles into official regulation in 2015?
3. The internet is a "vital service," but should it be a utility?

"The Tangled Web of Net Neutrality and Regulation," by Larry Downes, Harvard Business School Publishing, March 31, 2017. Reprinted by permission.

Net neutrality is a basic, but notoriously squishy, principle. It means that a broadband internet provider should not block, slow, or otherwise unfairly discriminate against any websites or online services. Despite being a simple idea, net neutrality has proven difficult to translate into US policy. It sits uncomfortably at the intersection of highly technical internet architecture and equally complex principles of administrative law. Even the term "net neutrality" was coined not by an engineer but by a legal academic, in 2003.

Since Donald Trump's election, the rhetoric surrounding net neutrality's imminent demise has been frenzied. Every move by newly appointed Federal Communications Commission (FCC) chair Ajit Pai generates a chorus of consumer advocates bemoaning the death of neutrality and the "end of the internet as we know it." Businesses and consumers are being warned that Republican lawmakers are united in their determination to not just modify the FCC's 2015 Open Internet Order, but to "kill," "destroy," "dismantle," or "abolish," the open internet, as soon as possible.

In the interest of exploring these issues, I've compiled some of the most important questions about net neutrality and the 2015 order, which grounded the rules in 1930s-era public utility law. To be clear, I agree with Netflix CEO Reed Hastings, who recently acknowledged that net neutrality principles have been and will continue to be strictly enforced not by regulation but by powerful market forces. My view is pretty simple: Most efforts to regulate the internet make things worse in the long term—or, in this case, much sooner. Here, the effort to transform Internet Service Providers (ISPs) into utilities is a cure far worse than the problem.

Let's start with the key players. First, there's the FCC, which along with other, sometimes rival, agencies, including the Federal Trade Commission (FTC), represents the main US regulatory bodies for internet usage. There's the president, who appoints the members of the Commissions, and Congress, which is solely responsible for delegating legislative authority to them.

Then there are the businesses in the internet ecosystem, often unhelpfully divided into "edge providers," such as Google, Facebook, and Netflix, and "infrastructure" providers, including engineering groups, ISPs, and companies that support the backbone of the internet. (Increasingly, the distinction is meaningless.) And, as with other issues, there are DC-based advocacy groups, regularly quoted in the press, many of which have with strong pro- or anti-regulatory biases.

Next, it's important to understand the 2015 Open Internet Order. This is an FCC rule, advocated for by President Obama, that based new net neutrality rules on old public utility laws originally written to regulate the former Bell telephone monopoly. The 2015 order mostly addressed a radical policy shift from competing private networks to public utility treatment for broadband, or "reclassification," with authority to enforce net neutrality being a mere side effect.

The order passed, in early 2015, by a party-line vote of 3–2. (Pai was one of the commissioners who voted against it. More on that later.) At the time, advocates hailed reclassification as a necessary foundation for net neutrality. But reclassification, separate from the net neutrality rules themselves, was less popular with broadband providers, which, along with leading internet engineering groups and companies like Google and Netflix, were concerned that the FCC would use the broad public utility powers it granted itself to regulate the internet well beyond enforcing net neutrality.

If the FCC or Congress revises or even reverses the public utility order, isn't that the end of net neutrality? No. The Open Internet principles (as the FCC has always referred to net neutrality) long predate the 2015 Order. When a court found in 2010 that the FCC lacked authority to enforce them, the agency formalized them as rules. The same court rejected that effort in 2014, however, concluding that the agency had failed to identify a source of legal authority from Congress, precipitating the 2015 Order.

Thus, for most of the history of the commercial internet, there have never been formal net neutrality rules. Still, during a decade of largely inside-the-Beltway squabbling, the FCC has only once identified a violation of the principles that might have been barred by any version of its rules.

That may be in large part because, even without the FCC, the kinds of behavior net neutrality prohibits are either counterproductive for broadband providers to engage in or are already illegal under anti-competition laws actively enforced by the Federal Trade Commission.

If the FTC was already the internet's "cop on the beat," why does the FCC also need to regulate? In part, the net neutrality fight has always been an inter-agency power struggle, with the FTC and the FCC each determined to establish new relevance in the emerging internet ecosystem. One (perhaps) unintended consequence, however, of the reclassification of broadband as a public utility is that the FCC explicitly cut off the jurisdiction of the FTC, which can't oversee utilities. Reversing reclassification but preserving the net neutrality rules—an action now being considered at the FCC and in Congress—would restore oversight to both agencies.

But the internet is a "vital service," isn't it? Why shouldn't it be a utility? Without doubt, our broadband infrastructure has become critical to business and consumers alike as a leading source of economic growth and productivity. But the legal designation of a "public utility" is more than just an acknowledgment of that importance. For over a century, economists have long cautioned that treating infrastructure as a quasi-public monopoly should only be considered a last resort to overcome severe market failings.

That's because utility treatment comes at a high cost. A monopoly or municipal utility, by definition, doesn't compete with anyone, eliminating incentives for investment, innovation, customer service, and maintenance. The sad state of most US power, water, and mass transit systems painfully illustrates that point.

By comparison, private investors have spent nearly $1.5 trillion on competing wired and mobile broadband networks over the last 20 years, and are poised to accelerate their efforts if the utility classification is undone. Though consumers in rural and mountainous regions may not yet have the fastest speeds, and contrary to what utility advocates claim, US broadband deployment and pricing is the envy of much of the rest of the world.

So if the public utility order is reversed, how will net neutrality be preserved? There are several options. The FCC could, for example, revise the 2015 order along the lines of a 2014 court ruling that even former FCC Chairman Tom Wheeler initially referred to as his "roadmap"—although that would only defer the possibility of reclassification until the next administration. Inconsistency would depress business investment, which nobody wants.

The better solution would be to make the net neutrality rules a matter of federal law. And that is exactly what House and Senate Republicans proposed in late 2014. The chairmen of the congressional commerce committees, with FCC oversight, jointly introduced a bill that codified much stronger net neutrality rules even than those the FCC approved in its 2010 effort. The Republican bill, for example, would have preemptively banned ISPs from blocking websites, slowing traffic, or offering prioritization for content as a paid service (so-called "fast lanes").

That bill also made clear that Congress never intended the FCC to have the discretion to transform broadband into a public utility at will, and in doing so subject it to rate regulation and other micromanagement. But since Democrats expected to win the White House in the 2016 election, they showed no interest in the bill, confident that an FCC chaired by someone Hillary Clinton picked would support the 2015 Order. Even since Trump's election, Republicans have made clear that a potential bi-partisan compromise on this matter is still on the table.

Broadband ISPs will never go along with such a law, will they? They will. ISPs are as unhappy about the endless uncertainty around net neutrality as anyone, and support a permanent legislative solution. While some providers have objected to the particular wording of some of the rules in the past, they don't object to net neutrality. Indeed, they practiced it during nearly two decades when the FCC had no rules requiring them to do so.

Verizon was actually the only broadband provider to challenge the 2010 version of the rules, and then only on very technical legal grounds. In ongoing litigation over the 2015 Public Utility Order, other ISPs have challenged the substance and process of reclassification, but, again, not the rules themselves.

Verizon, whose business model has changed substantially since 2010, now supports aspects of the 2015 Order with which even some of the advocacy groups took issue. And both Comcast and AT&T remain subject to slightly different versions of the rules regardless of what happens to the 2015 Order, having committed to them as conditions for recent mergers.

This brings us back to President Trump: Didn't he promise to end net neutrality? Not exactly. Some people are seizing on a single tweet from 2014, before Trump was even a candidate, in which he referred to net neutrality as President Obama's "top down power grab." That comment (his only one I'm aware of on the subject) came the day after a White House demand that led to the 2015 reclassification—the actual source of Trump's objection. Since then, he has said nothing.

At best, Trump's position on (and interest in) net neutrality is unclear. And having now appointed Pai as the new Chairman of the FCC, Trump has little direct influence over the Commission which, by law, operates as an independent expert agency. Pai, who has been involved with the FCC most of his professional life, is already working to improve the agency's transparency and predictability.

But Chairman Pai is a net neutrality "foe," isn't he? Pai objected strongly to reclassification of the internet as utility, but he has always been a supporter of net neutrality principles. Before and since becoming Chairman, Pai has repeatedly pledged to protect the core ideas behind net neutrality, including, as he describes them, "The freedom to access lawful content, the freedom to use applications, the freedom to attach personal devices to the network, and the freedom to obtain service plan information."

A frequently misquoted 2016 promise by Pai to take a "weed whacker" to outdated FCC regulations had nothing to do with net neutrality and, indeed, echoed multiple executive orders issued by Presidents Obama and Clinton requiring agency heads to retire obsolete federal rules that remain on the books.

Pai did vote against the 2015 Order, but his dissent was almost entirely devoted to the legal and economic risks of public utility reclassification, as well as the irregular process by which the agency substituted the White House plan for Wheeler's original "roadmap."

Don't edge providers like Google and Netflix, as well as start-ups, rely on net neutrality? Advocates for expanded public utility regulation of broadband providers are busy conjuring worst-case scenarios for any change to the 2015 Order, insisting for example that ISPs will immediately begin charging content providers such as Google and Netflix special fees to deliver information to their subscribers, and otherwise destroy the equal playing field by which internet services can be accessed by consumers.

These predictions intentionally ignore technical, business, and legal realities, however, that make such fees unlikely, if not impossible. For one thing, in the last two decades, during which no net neutrality rules were in place, ISPs have never found a business case for squeezing the Open Internet. In part, that's the result of intense competitive pressure among mobile providers and increasingly between mobile and wired ISPs. In broadband, it's the content providers who have leverage over the ISPs and not the other way around, as Netflix recently acknowledged in brushing aside concern about any "weakening" of net neutrality rules.

This might be why neither Google nor Netflix thought the public utility reclassification was a good idea. Former Google CEO Eric Schmidt argued against it at the time, saying he was worried that reclassification meant "starting to regulate an awful lot of things on the Internet," a concern shared by the Internet Society and other non-partisan engineering groups. Netflix, recognizing that public utility regulations for broadband could someday extend to their own non-neutral conduct, reconsidered its own advocacy after the 2015 Order was passed.

A frequently misunderstood point is that Netflix's intervention late in the fight over the 2015 Order was not about avoiding future fees for last-mile delivery of its content. The company instead asked the FCC to mandate free interconnection for its wholesale traffic partners and its own content delivery networks embedded throughout ISP facilities—something the company confusingly called "strong" net neutrality.

Despite claims that Netflix traffic was being "throttled" by ISPs, slowdowns in Netflix traffic in 2014 (which gained extra attention following comedian John Oliver's famous rant about the issue) turned out to be the fault of one of Netflix's own transit providers. The transit provider was over capacity and had reduced service at peak times to wholesale customers, like Netflix, without telling anyone. Netflix actually pays below market rates for interconnection—costs so small they don't even show up in financial statements.

The FCC declined to extend "neutrality" to the core of the network in its 2015 Order, and Netflix quickly lost interest in the debate.

Should business leaders intervene to preserve net neutrality? The kind of full-scale resistance that utility advocates are now calling for in a renewed net neutrality battle would be deeply misguided and counter-productive, especially if directed at the FCC and Chairman Pai. As noted, the agency bases its regulatory decisions on actual economic and technical analysis and not advocacy, no matter how spirited. Admittedly that hasn't always been the case, particularly in the last several years, but Pai has committed to restoring the commission's own neutrality.

What business leaders inside and outside the internet ecosystem can and should do, however, is to encourage Congress to act once and for all, protecting the open internet while preserving an investment environment essential for continued broadband expansion and improvement. It's hard to imagine anyone disagreeing with that objective, or with a lasting solution to a problem that has plagued regulators and industry alike for too long.

Congress and the FCC are already working to determine the most effective steps both to undo the public utility reclassification and put the net neutrality principles on solid legal ground once and for all. Watch for FCC action and revised legislation that would do just that sometime in the next few months.

> *"When the Court ruled on behalf of the FCC and net neutrality, it was a major victory for the public against extraordinarily powerful corporate interests."*

The Fight for a Free Internet Is Akin to the Civil Rights Movement

Lori McGlinchey

In the following viewpoint, Lori McGlinchey provides a reaction piece to the news of the US Court of Appeals decision to uphold the FCC's net neutrality regulations, which were passed in 2015. The author compares the fight for a free and open internet with the civil rights movement of the 1960s and also details how important the efforts of grassroots organizations toward the preservation of these regulations are. With the establishment of these regulations, the author maintains that it is possible to move forward with continuing to expand internet access and make it even more affordable. McGlinchey is the senior program officer for internet freedom at the Ford Foundation.

As you read, consider the following questions:

1. Why are internet rights and civil rights so closely intertwined?
2. What was one of the most significant factors in the US Court of Appeals upholding the net neutrality regulations?
3. Is it possible to expand internet infrastructure with net neutrality?

The verdict is in: The Internet is not a luxury. Broadband is an essential public utility, and must be equally accessible to everyone.

Yesterday, the US Court of Appeals for the District of Columbia Circuit ruled decisively to uphold the Federal Communications Commission's net neutrality rules, which require Internet service providers to treat all web traffic equally—preventing them from blocking or slowing some traffic and offering preferential treatment to sites that pay for faster service. Net neutrality is essential because it maintains the Internet as an open platform for free expression, political engagement, education, and economic opportunity.

As the *New York Times* explained in an op-ed, "The decision helps to ensure a level playing field for smaller and start-up Internet businesses because it precludes larger, established companies like Amazon and Netflix from simply paying broadband companies for faster delivery. Equally important, it ensures reliable service and choice for consumers by acknowledging that the internet, now a requisite of modern life, is akin to a utility, subject to regulation in the public interest."

How Did We Get Here?

In February 2015, the Federal Communications Commission voted to reclassify broadband service under Title II of the Communications Act—affirming that the Internet is an essential public service, and so the rules that govern its provision must treat it as such.

Channeling John Oliver, I will admit that even I find myself nodding off as I type the sentence "reclassify broadband service under Title II of the Communications Act." So why should we care about that 2015 FCC vote to do just that, and yesterday's court decision upholding that vote?

Even if the terms we use to describe this work—net neutrality, Title II, reclassification—are dry, the real world consequences of an open Internet are profoundly important. The Ford Foundation and the organizations we support, in every field, depend on the existence of an open, democratic communications infrastructure. Explaining the deep connection between Internet rights and civil rights, Ford Foundation president Darren Walker explained, "The Internet is now our central platform for engaging in dialogue about the most important issues facing our country. It's where we share our views, speak out against injustice, and express our hopes for the future."

After the FCC's 2015 vote to enact strong net neutrality rules, cable, telecom, and wireless Internet providers sued to overturn these regulations, arguing that the rules would constrain business. Yesterday, when the Court ruled on behalf of the FCC and net neutrality, it was a major victory for the public against extraordinarily powerful corporate interests.

Advocates Explain Why Net Neutrality Matters

For more than a decade, the organizations we support have been working tirelessly on what has until recently been a fairly obscure topic, even as the Internet has assumed an increasingly central role in our lives. Responding to yesterday's victory, Rashad Robinson, executive director of ColorOfChange, emphasized the importance of net neutrality for black communities. "Net neutrality is essential to protecting our free and open Internet, which has been crucial to modern-day civil rights movements and fights for equality," he said. "Our ability to have our voices heard in this democracy depends on an open Internet because it allows voices and ideas to spread based on substance, rather than financial backing."

Malkia Cyril, executive director of the Center for Media Justice (who writes so powerfully about digital black power in the 21st century), connected the importance of net neutrality to the tragedy dominating the news. "Those who lost their lives at the Pulse nightclub shooting in Orlando, most of whom were Black and Latino, are 49 of the many reasons we celebrate the court's decision to keep the Internet open," she said. "With a truly open Internet, we can hear the voices of those who lost loved ones, organize vigils nationwide to honor their passing, oppose the hateful rhetoric that compromises democracy, and organize to prevent this from ever happening again."

Michael Scurato, vice president of policy at the National Hispanic Media Coalition, explained why the ruling matters in a broad context. "This decision is a decisive victory for those who rely on the open Internet to express themselves, organize, make a living, participate in policymaking, get a job, earn an education and do all of the critical things that we so often take for granted," he said. "Hopefully, rather than continuing to fight this losing battle against openness, entrepreneurship and innovation, opponents will now turn to constructive endeavors, like making sure that everyone in this country can access affordable broadband."

More than a year ago, after the initial FCC vote, Harold Feld, senior vice president at Public Knowledge, described how a powerful communications body came to affirm the importance of an open Internet. It happened, he explained, "because hundreds of lawyers, grassroots organizers, and policy advocates persuaded over 4 million people to stand up for their rights and demand that the government act to protect them from the unrestrained corporate power of broadband access providers. It shows—to everyone's surprise—that government of the people, by the people and for the people has not perished from this Earth."

Free Press president Craig Aaron also underscored the importance of grassroots efforts in making sure that judgment was upheld. "The real story here was dozens of public interest groups, new civil rights leaders and netroots organizers coordinating actions online and off, inside and outside Washington," he said. "Artists, musicians, faith leaders and legal scholars bolstered their efforts. And about a dozen mostly unsung advocates in DC pushed back daily against the phone and cable lobby. This diverse coalition broke the FCC's website, jammed switchboards on Capitol Hill, and forged new alliances that are transforming how telecom and technology policy is made."

What's Next?

Strong net neutrality rules in the US ensure that we will continue to have access to a free and open Internet—one that will remain an engine of free expression, economic growth, and innovation. With those protections in place, we're continuing to work with our partners to make the Internet more accessible and affordable—so that everyone can tap into the benefits and extraordinary potential this court decision helps protect.

> "*In 2014, the FCC was flooded
> with some 4 million comments in
> response to a proposal to allow
> paid prioritization.*"

Many Internet Companies Fight to Keep Net Neutrality Rules

Alina Selukh

In the following viewpoint, Alina Selukh previews a planned digital protest in July 2017, called the Day of Action, which expressed dissatisfaction with the FCC's plans to roll back regulations it placed on ISPs in 2015. Web companies have argued the importance of net neutrality rules so cable and telecom companies do not become gatekeepers of how Americans experience the internet, compared to how browsing is controlled in other countries. The writer also points out that major internet-based companies planned to participate in the event. Selukh is a business reporter at National Public Radio (NPR), where she follows the path of the retail and tech industries.

As you read, consider the following questions:

1. Which companies participated in the 2017 Day of Action protests in favor of net neutrality?
2. Why is the topic of paid prioritization the most prevalent topic in the argument for net neutrality?
3. Why would ISPs support the principles of net neutrality but not the regulations passed by the FCC?

I f the activists' predictions pan out, Wednesday might see one of the largest digital protests to date.

Dozens of websites and apps have joined ranks with consumer advocacy groups, through a "Day of Action," to publicly protest the plan by the Federal Communications Commission to roll back regulations it placed on Internet service providers in 2015.

The rules enforce the principle called net neutrality—that Internet service providers shouldn't slow down or block any sites or apps, or otherwise decide what content gets to users faster. The FCC, under Chairman Ajit Pai, is weighing whether (and how) to undo the rules that enforced net neutrality by placing Internet providers under the strictest-ever FCC oversight.

At the time, Pai was a dissenting Republican commissioner on the Democrat-majority FCC. Now, the party control has reversed and President Trump has elevated him to chairman. Pai has presented the net neutrality rules as the government becoming the regulator of the Internet. He has argued that the rules have put a "bureaucratic straitjacket" on the telecom industry, slowing investments in the expansion of broadband access and innovation.

Numerous Web companies, for their part, have argued that net neutrality rules are paramount to ensure that cable and telecom companies don't become the gatekeepers of how Americans experience the Internet—what people can access at what speeds. The Internet Association, the trade group for Internet companies, says investments have not slowed.

"We haven't actually lived in a world where fully the ISPs could block access," says Denelle Dixon, chief legal and business officer at Mozilla. "It's very hard to imagine a world without (net neutrality). This is the world we need to imagine now."

Wednesday's "Day Of Action" is an Internet protest, during which scores of websites and apps are planning to feature banners, pop-ups or other alerts—like the perpetually spinning wheel—all to encourage users to reach out to the FCC or Congress in favor of the existing rules.

Participants are expected to include Netflix, Etsy, Vimeo, Twitter, Reddit and Amazon. Google and Facebook have recently said they plan to participate as well. Organizers include advocacy groups Fight for the Future, Demand Progress and Free Press— some of the same activists who organized online campaigns to push the Obama-era FCC toward strict net neutrality regulations and, years earlier, the epic blackout to boycott anti-piracy bills known as SOPA and PIPA.

The FCC is currently accepting public comment on its proposal to loosen the rules for Internet providers, which is titled "Restoring Internet Freedom." Pai's review of the rules asks wide-spanning questions, proposing a looser regulatory scheme for Internet service providers as well as seeking comment on whether net neutrality principles should be adopted to begin with.

One key element at stake is the idea of paid prioritization, which would give Internet providers the ability to strike deals with content companies to give some apps and websites—or their own services—special treatment.

This is particularly a sensitive matter to Vimeo, a video service smaller than Google's YouTube or other companies that offer video like Netflix, Amazon and now Facebook. Vimeo's general counsel Michael Cheah says paid prioritization would "cable-ize the Internet" and hurt independent and small creators.

"Any time you have a situation where there's an additional barrier to entry, an additional cost you pay someone or toll you

FAKE SUPPORT?

AT&T has a surprise for tech firms and internet activists supporting net neutrality, the principle that bars internet service providers from playing favorites with websites and apps.

Although AT&T has fiercely fought the Federal Communications Commission's net-neutrality rules, it's backing Wednesday's "day of action" denouncing AT&T and other ISPs.

Of course, AT&T doesn't actually agree with the aim of the protest—to support the 2015 regulation that the FCC wants to overturn now that Republicans are in charge.

AT&T says it supports an "open internet" and believes companies shouldn't block web content or slow down videos from other providers. Rather, AT&T says it merely opposes the FCC rules that set it in place. Comcast and Verizon joined AT&T in making that distinction. ISPs don't like the FCC's approach because it treats internet service as a utility and comes with more oversight. They worry about price regulation and say the rules hurt broadband investment.

Tim Karr, the campaign director for Free Press, an advocacy group that supports net neutrality, slammed the ISPs for "simply attempting to fake the funk, pretending to support net neutrality while opposing the (FCC) rules that make it an enforceable reality."

The 2015 regulation is the only set of net-neutrality rules that courts have upheld.

Internet activists and tech firms hope that the protest will pressure Congress and the FCC, the way a highly visible 2012 online protest—including the blackout of Wikipedia's English-language site for 24 hours—helped kill anti-piracy legislation that tech companies equated to internet censorship.

This year's online protest is more muted. Netflix put a gray banner at the top of its home page and is tweeting out "gif" animations in support. Amazon's website has a small square inviting users to "learn more." Twitter is promoting "net neutrality" as the top trending topic in the US. Google tweeted a blog post. Smaller tech companies including Airbnb and Etsy have fat banners on their home pages.

Karr said that internet users have taken "hundreds of thousands of actions," like contacting the FCC. There had been about 6 million filings on net neutrality's overturn made to the FCC as of Tuesday night, both supporting and opposing the policy; that had risen to 6.7 million Wednesday afternoon.

"ISPs Surprise Net Neutrality Fans on Protest Day," Tali Arbel, Phys.org, July 12, 2017.

have to get on the road," he says, "it's going to favor a type of content that already has a footing in the market."

Critics of net neutrality rules have argued that some such paid-prioritization deals might, in fact, serve the users best—and that the FCC's approach shouldn't be definitive and prescriptive.

Comcast, Verizon and other large providers have said they do support the net neutrality principles of no blocking and no throttling, but oppose the regulatory structure imposed by the 2015 rules. It reclassified the Internet as a more heavily regulated "telecommunications service" rather than an "information service" under the Title II of the Communications Act.

AT&T and telecom trade groups have since lost a court challenge to the Title II approach, but they are expected to seek a Supreme Court review of the matter. Pai wants to undo the Title II reclassification, which the industry argues has burdened them. Net neutrality advocates say without the Title II structure, the FCC can't really enforce net neutrality.

In 2014, the FCC was flooded with some 4 million comments in response to a proposal to allow paid prioritization. John Oliver's late-night comedy episode on net neutrality also targeted the FCC. But this time around, Pai and his fellow Republican commissioner at the FCC have called for comments to present a cost-benefit analysis or be otherwise "evidence-based."

In a May 2017 meeting, as we reported, Commissioner Mike O'Rielly said:

"Thankfully, our rulemaking proceeding is not decided like a *Dancing With The Stars* contest, since counts of comments submitted have only so much value," O'Rielly said, adding: "Instead of operating an economics-free zone where the benefits of the rules are assumed to outweigh any cost, commenters will need to provide evidence to support their arguments that the rules are or are not needed."

Vimeo's Cheah says this approach is unfair given the broad scope of the proposal itself. "The idea that you don't have the right to file a comment if you don't know the 'magic words'" like Title II, he says, "frankly, it's insulting."

As the net neutrality policy debate stretches into its second decade, lawmakers in Congress have also spoken about settling it with a new law.

Some of the participants in Wednesday's "Day of Action" say the protest aims to pressure lawmakers to stand up in support of the current rules, possibly more so than trying to sway the FCC.

Free-market groups and other critics of the current regulations are also looking to Congress as a place to settle the net neutrality debate.

"Enthusiasm for Title II regulations for the internet is misplaced," wrote a PR firm representing the Internet-provider trade group Broadband for America. "Activists should work together with others who favor net neutrality to get bipartisan legislation through Congress that all sides can agree upon."

The FCC is collecting public comments until July 17. Then it will collect replies to comments until Aug. 16.

> *"Chairman Pai's early actions are not consistent with those of an agency trying to protect consumers."*

Our First Amendment Rights Are at Stake

Brett Kokinadis

In the following viewpoint, Brett Kokinadis criticizes anti–net neutrality actions taken by FCC chair Ajit Pai and the Republican-controlled Congress. While Pai claims the anti–net neutrality decisions will promote consumer choice and innovation, the Pai-led FCC stopped an investigation into "zero rating," which is popular with low-income households but could set a problematic precedent for the future of an open and free internet. The Senate passed a law that would stop the FCC from ruling on ISPs selling data logs of consumers' personal internet usage. Kokinadis is chief operating officer of the Party of Reason and Progress.

As you read, consider the following questions:

1. Why would FCC chair Pai's actions be seen as inconsistent with protecting consumer interests?
2. What are the benefits of a level playing field for start-ups entering the ISP market?
3. What is "zero rating"?

On February 26, 2015, the FCC enacted landmark regulations to preserve Net Neutrality. The new regulations put in place

"Challenges to Net Neutrality," The Party of Reason and Progress, July 13, 2017. Reprinted by permission.

a number of consumer protections preventing Internet Service Providers from blocking access to websites, throttling traffic based on application, origin, or content, and outlawing paid prioritization. These regulations help preserve the internet as an open platform, allowing consumers to access its vast wealth of information at will, ensuring a level playing field for businesses and promoting a universal service.

The 2015 regulations have faced legal challenges and, so far, have been upheld. However, the Trump administration poses a new threat to net neutrality in the form of FCC chairman Ajit Pai. Pai has recently announced a plan to repeal the Obama-era net neutrality regulations with support from Republican lawmakers. Additionally, Chairman Pai's early actions are not consistent with those of an agency trying to protect consumers.

Pai has rescinded an expansion of the FCC lifeline program that allowed for low income households to receive discounted broadband service. Under his guidance, the FCC also halted an investigation into the practice of "zero rating" that, while popular with some consumers, may present a threat to competing start-ups entering the market. Without a level playing field, small internet startups will struggle to overcome the advantages that the current dominant tech companies can potentially acquire from further partnering directly with large service providers.

Pai, formerly in the employ of Verizon, is an open critic of Net Neutrality. His arguments mostly hinge on the suggestion that such rules are unnecessary and that consumer demand will continue to preserve today's open internet. While that has largely been the case to date, there have been past incidents of throttling bandwidth for certain applications, language included in the terms of service that bans residential users from setting up home WiFi networks, and bans on customers using Virtual Private Networks (page 17) to protect their privacy online. This caused enough concern over the subject to warrant regulations being put in place to prevent consumer abuse and protect our access to an open internet.

A first step in attacking net neutrality and consumer choice, Senate Joint Resolution 34, has been signed into law. This resolution not only blocked an impending rule that would prevent your internet service provider (ISP) from selling data logs of your internet usage, but also prevents the FCC from making any rule on the matter in the future. While proponents of this bill claim that the FCC regulations were unnecessary and unfair to ISPs, critics noted that current Federal Trade Commission privacy rules have been inadequate in the past. Additionally, consumers have some control over what information is handed to online content providers that sell information, such as Facebook or Google, while their ISP handles all of their online traffic without exception.

If net neutrality regulations are repealed ISPs would have significantly more power to enforce bans on using VPNs, TOR browsers and other privacy-protecting applications, forcing users to allow the full disclosure of personal information or browsing habits any time they use the internet. Traffic could be blocked based on application, geography or content as an ISP sees fit. Since consumers sometimes have limited choice in ISPs, this could create a situation where people are forced to allow their internet usage to be monitored, unable to use an application of their choice, or even be prevented from telecommuting or working from home through a VPN.

Without net neutrality, there would be nothing to prevent the internet from being sold in packages similar to cable television plans dependent upon the goodwill of ISPs. The concept of "zero rating" that was to be reviewed by the FCC is an example of how such packaging could be introduced. Zero rating allows cellular consumers to access content from popular online services without using data from the monthly allotment purchased with their cellular plan. Under this type of plan, all services not included in the zero rating list are effectively pay per view, or pay per use, whatever the case may be. The only difference between a zero rating scheme and pay-per-view cable is that rather than paying just before each viewing or usage, a zero rating scheme simply charges customers for an agreed upon amount of usage each month which the customer can then spend on whatever content they wish.

While this may be beneficial to consumers who only use today's most popular services, it would make starting a new online venture extremely difficult, hurt consumers who use less popular services, and could lead to severe market stagnation. Unless a company has enough start-up capital to pay whatever fee a provider charges to have their service zero rated, breaking into the growing mobile app market may be impossible.

Pai has claimed that all of the FCC's recent anti-neutrality decisions will promote consumer choice and lower prices through innovation driven by market competition, yet he opposed the removal of rules protecting ISPs from having to compete with local providers that directly limited consumer choice. And while there are downsides to forbidding paid prioritization of content, it is shortsighted to claim this is the only solution to network congestion or that only an unregulated market will lead to innovation. Revoking the current common carrier status of service providers means they would no longer be required to provide equal access under the US Code, allowing ISPs to deny access for any reason they deemed necessary. This will further limit consumers' ability to freely use the internet.

The internet is becoming increasingly vital for not just business, but daily life and education as well. Rather than protecting consumers, the FCC under this administration has already put children of low-income parents at risk academically. Getting rid of net neutrality does nothing to provide additional choice, gives no guarantees of reduced costs and actively puts consumers at risk of identity fraud and scams. There has been no indication that Pai is interested in seeing the internet being used as anything other than a paid content delivery service similar to cable television.

Net neutrality is about far more than just how quickly smaller websites load. Our First Amendment rights, privacy, economic freedom, and the future of our children's education are all dependent on a free and open internet.

Periodical and Internet Sources Bibliography

The following articles have been selected to supplement the diverse views presented in this chapter.

Kevin Collier, "The Nightmare Scenario of an America Without Net Neutrality," *Week*, March 11, 2017. http://theweek.com/articles /682660/nightmare-scenario-america-without-net-neutrality.

Federal Communications Commission, "Protecting and Promoting the Open Internet," *Federal Register*, December 21, 2016. https:// www.federalregister.gov/documents/2016/12/21/2016-30766 /protecting-and-promoting-the-open-internet.

Brett M. Frischmann and Barbara van Scheik, "Network Neutrality and the Economics of an Information Superhighway: A Reply to Professor Yoo," *Jurimetrics Journal*, 2007. https://cyberlaw .stanford.edu/files/publication/files/vanschewick-2007 -networkneutrality-economics-of-info-superhighway.pdf.

Brian Fung, "Verizon and Comcast Are Working to Prevent State-Level Net Neutrality Rules," *Los Angeles Times*, November 6, 2017. http://beta.latimes.com/business/technology/la-fi-net -neutrality-20171106-story.html.

John Herrman, "Welcome to the Net Neutrality Nightmare Scenario," BuzzFeed, January 14, 2014. https://www.buzzfeed .com/jwherrman/welcome-to-the-net-neutrality-nightmare -scenario?utm_term=.vyglOVgpm#.urVE3pn7z.

Cecilia Kang, "Verizon Sues FCC over Net Neutrality Rules," *Washington Post*, September 30, 2011. https://www .washingtonpost.com/blogs/post-tech/post/verizon-sues-fcc -over-net-neutrality-rules/2011/09/30/gIQAFUP0AL_blog .html?utm_term=.09da5ddc2b62.

Milton Mueller and Hadi Asghari, "Deep Packet Inspection and Bandwidth Management: Battles over Bittorrent in Canada and the United States," TPRC 2011, January 24, 2012. https://papers .ssrn.com/sol3/papers.cfm?abstract_id=1989644.

On the Media, "Net Neutrality and You," WNYC, January 16, 2014. https://www.wnyc.org/story/end-net-neutrality?tab=transcript.

Nilay Patel, "Everything Verizon Says in This Terrible Video About Net Neutrality vs. the Truth," Verge, May 2, 2017. https://www

.theverge.com/2017/5/2/15520818/verizon-net-neutrality-craig
-silliman-truth.

Brad Reed, "Cable Companies' 'Comically Profitable' Margins Said
to Provide Little Incentive to Invest in Fiber," BGR, February 6,
2013. http://bgr.com/2013/02/06/cable-company-internet
-service-margins-316532/.

Jeff Sommer, "What Net Neutrality Rules Say," *New York
Times*, March 12, 2015. https://www.nytimes.com
/interactive/2015/03/12/technology/net-neutrality-rules
-explained.html.

Tim Wu, "Network Neutrality, Broadband Discrimination," *Journal
of Telecommunications and High Technology Law* 2, June 5, 2005.
https://papers.ssrn.com/sol3/papers.cfm?abstract_id=388863.

Edward Wyatt, "Rebuffing F.C.C. in 'Net Neutrality' Case, Court
Allows Streaming Deals," *New York Times*, January 14, 2014.
https://www.nytimes.com/2014/01/15/technology/appeals-court
-rejects-fcc-rules-on-internet-service-providers.html.

OPPOSING
VIEWPOINTS®
SERIES

CHAPTER 4

Is It Necessary to Have a Free and Open Internet in the United States?

Chapter Preface

The following chapter offers insights into the guarantees of free speech in the United States and gives further insights into net neutrality regulations in other areas like India and the European Union. The chapter also shows the kind of internet restrictions found in single-party-led countries like the People's Republic of China, with its Communist Party.

Free speech as we know it in the United States does not exist in countries like China, where the internet is restricted by firewalls and state-sponsored censorship that make it difficult for users to access the internet via a virtual private network (VPN) or even the web offered by the government. In the United States, the American Civil Liberties Union gives historical context to the earliest days of the argument over a free and open internet and how American liberties cannot be valued if they are controlled by entities with their own agendas, like private companies that may prefer to offer easier access to websites that share their political view.

Considerations for the ultimate benefit of protection must be the consumer, and whether the most powerful members of the ruling parties agree or not, the American public has made it clear in recent years that it favors net neutrality regulation, which brings rise to the question of for whom people like FCC chair Ajit Pai are working. The Party of Reason and Progress, as cited in a viewpoint in this chapter, questions if the Republican-led FCC in 2017 is actively working in the interest of the consumer, and if not, for whom is it working? Do the net neutrality regulations truly have a negative impact on smaller ISPs, or is that a fiction that has been thoroughly debunked yet is still used by those who feel the message fits their narrative?

> *"There are now hundreds of newspapers with strong linguistic and regional differences, where, under commercial pressures, the likes and dislikes of readers have grown more important than the Party's instructions."*

Fear of the Internet and Free Speech Has Serious Consequences

Giovanni Navarria

In the following viewpoint, Giovanni Navarria offers a bleak look into the potential future of a government-regulated internet that is censored and strictly policed. The People's Republic of China is solely governed by the Chinese Communist Party, which is built on a foundation of arbitrary power and, among other things, strict control of communication and media. The growth of digital communications around the world makes government control increasingly difficult, especially with the expanded availability of VPNs, and even with government-sponsored censorship—including the "Golden Shield," also called the "Great Firewall of China"—the Chinese government has a complex relationship with the internet and the quality it allows to be available to its citizens. Navarria is a research fellow of the Sydney Democracy Network at the University of Sydney.

Navarria, Giovanni (2016), To Censor or Not to Censor: Roots, Current Trends and the Long-Term Consequences of the Chinese Communist Party's Fear of the Internet, *Communication, Politics and Culture*, 49(2), 82-110. https://www.rmit.edu.au/content/dam/rmit/documents/college-of-design-and-social-context/schools/media-and-communication/cpc-journal/volume-49-issue-2/CPC-Journal-49-2-Navarria.pdf. Licensed under CC BY-ND.

As you read, consider the following questions:

1. In countries with an open internet like the United States, why would users choose to use VPNs to access the internet instead of available ISPs?
2. What are the difficulties governments like China face when censoring the internet?
3. Why are there no real "live" broadcasts?

Introduction

Along with the Democratic People's Republic of Korea, the People's Republic of China now stands among the longest-lasting one-party regimes of modern times. The long-standing resilience of the Chinese Communist Party (CCP) is built on strong foundations: arbitrary power, indiscriminate use of violence, successful economic reforms, a weak rule of law and strict control of communication/media.

This article focuses on the latter point, the strict control of the media and communication. Specifically, my aim is to provide a new perspective on the role new communication modes play in the Beijing government's long-term survival strategy. Orthodox accounts of China's relationship with the media often emphasise its totalitarian elements, namely Chinese authorities' heavy use of censorship mechanisms to regulate what kind of information Chinese citizens receive. I do not attempt to challenge the fact that censorship and strict control of the media still play a crucial role in the authorities' exercise of power. I suggest, however, that the Party is slowly, but steadily changing tack. The Party's new approach is deep-rooted in the social and technological development of the last two decades. The constant and permeating spread of digital networked communication such as the internet and its many social media applications has, in fact, had a significant transformative effect on Chinese society. It has: introduced new businesses models, expanded its market, created new sources of revenue for both large and small businesses; reshaped its labour market and acted as the main engine of a vibrant and fast developing technology sector (Woetzel et al., 2014). Social media applications such as Tencent and WeChat have changed the way in which Chinese people buy goods, communicate with each other and generally live their daily lives (*The Economist*, 2016). More importantly, from the Party's perspective, the internet has transformed both people's attitude towards authority and the intricate dynamics of contestations of power. While citizens feel more empowered to openly criticize the government and its officials and question the validity of government policies, the growing complexity and fast-changing features of this new technological environment increase the Party's efforts "to find effective means to pursue old goals," such as "maintaining a monopoly on organized politics, limiting dissent, and censoring some ideas while privileging others" (Yang, Goldstein, and de Lisle, 2016, 3).

Paying particular attention to the threat digital storms and the spreading of internet rumours pose to the Party's monopoly of power, in the following pages I shed light on the reasons behind the Party's growing concern and outline the effects this has on the Party's approach to the internet and its relationship with Chinese citizens in an age dominated by digital communication networks. Considered in media terms, China is not straightforwardly a regime based on censorship. When we examine closely the heavily-contested field of digital networked media, we find the Party has been experimenting for some time with a variety of unusual democratic strategies, each of them designed to go beyond the need for censorship; each of them a new Party strategy to learn from its critics and win public consent for its rule. The first part of this work discusses the use of media as censorship tools, the second part elaborates on the changing attitudes of the Party towards digital networked media and what it means for its future.

State censorship of media has a long tradition in China: it dates as far back as the Qin dynasty when Emperor Qin Shi Huangdi (221–207 BCE) ordered the destruction of books written by his opponents (Confucius' texts, among many others, were considered subversive, hence banned and destroyed). More recently, in the early decades of the Republic of China, the persecution and imprisonment of journalists was the norm, rather than the exception, between 1911 and 1930, when many newspapers were closed and the few that survived the purge became mouthpieces for the regime (Lin 1936, pp. 167–70). During the 1930s the fate of journalists did not improve much under the rule of Chiang Kai-shek's Nationalist Party, the Kuomintang (KMT) (Hachten 2010, 20). But it was under Mao's leadership in 1949 that the state's approach became more totalitarian, with freedom of the press hitting its lowest point, with the media becoming the main apparatus of state propaganda. It became essential in spreading CCP ideology and policies; not only educating the masses, but also helping to organise and mobilise them (Lu 1979, 45). Not surprisingly, media outlets (especially newspapers) were never at liberty to criticise the state or report on unauthorised topics. Between 1958 and 1962, the years of the great famine, at least 45 million people reportedly starved to death in China (Dikötter 2010, pp. 324–34), yet the press remained silent about the victims and instead "exaggerated crop production" (Hachten, 2010, 21). After Mao's death in 1976 and the end of the Cultural Revolution, the mass communication system underwent a series of reforms. Although censorship did not disappear there were talks of press freedom and independence. The "honeymoon period" lasted just over a decade. The tragic ending to the student protest in Tiananmen Square in 1989 saw the Party shift its focus towards economic incentives to allow the market to flourish. But at the same time, it further restricted freedom of the press in political matters (Zhao, 1998, pp. 47–51). Ever since, China's media have been trapped in an apparent contradiction: variety of programming and audiences grow, but political freedom from state control and democratization of institutions is still absent. Overall, in political matters, all mainstream media can still be considered, to a great extent, mouthpieces for the Party.

The Publicity Department and the State Administration of Radio, Film, and Television have the last say on what kind of content can be broadcast to Chinese TV and radio audiences and the frequency and length of entertainment shows; they also instruct networks to give prominence to state-approved news items.

In China, there is no real "live" broadcasting because transmission delays are used to filter out possible damaging news items, especially when the Party is under pressure ("Radio journalist talks about censorship, delayed 'live' broadcasts" 2010).

Things are more complicated for newspapers: in recent years, the sector has undergone an economic boom, which has resulted in increased competition. There are now hundreds of newspapers with strong linguistic and regional differences, where, under commercial pressures, the likes and dislikes of readers have grown more important than the Party's instructions. The outcome of such a shift is, to some extent, extraordinary: despite Party controls, plenty of in-depth investigative journalism now happens in China (Bandurski and Hala, 2010).

Censoring the Internet

State controls in the field of digital communication media, yet the Party's attempt to exercise its censorious grip is proving to be far from straightforward. In 1995, when ChinaNet, the first internet service provider (ISP) in the country, was officially launched, it provided a few select users with a limited range of basic services, such as email, web surfing and newsgroup and chat rooms (Zhou, 2006 pp. 135–38). Since then, helped by government planning, the field of digital communications has expanded at a remarkable pace. There are now more than 700 million users spending on average of over 26 hours per week online, more time than on any other medium. They use the web for a growing variety of activities, such as instant messaging (86%); accessing news (79.6%); listening to music (73.4%) and as blog/personal space (70.7%). Microblog sites and social networking sites, such as WeChat and Sina Corporation's Weibo (like Twitter), are at about 45 per cent usage (Xinhua News,

2016; "Statistical Report on Internet Development in China 35th Report" 2015).

The Party's desire to promote "indigenous innovation," to only use technologies manufactured by home-grown companies, rather than being reliant on foreign manufacturers, has helped make Chinese technology companies such as Lenovo, Huawei and Xiaomi major competitors in global communications markets. The Party's stated goal is for China to become an "innovation oriented society" by 2020 and a "world leader in science and technology" by 2050 (Bichler and Schmidkonz, 2012; Cao, Suttmeier, and Simon, 2009; Kennedy, Suttmeier, and Su, 2008). In support of a rapidly expanding service-driven economy, the government has committed staggering sums (US$182 billion by the end of 2017). China is now the leading online retail market (and, at the end of 2014, Alibaba, China's largest e-commerce company, overtook Wal-Mart Stores as the world's largest retailer).

These efforts have also been a boon for employment, with experts forecasting the growth of 3.5 million new internet-based job opportunities by 2020 (China Daily, 2015; "Statistical Report on Internet Development in China 35th Report" 2015).

From the Party's perspective, these statistics are dazzling and worrying at the same time: on the one hand the internet brings the Party closer to its citizens (for instance, it enhances communication between officials and citizens and speeds up authorities' response-time to issues of public concern); on the other hand, it can have destructive effects on the Party's vision to make China a "harmonious society" (héxié shèhuì) (Chan, 2010). Hu Jintao, during his time as the General Secretary of the Communist Party (2002–2012), raised the alarm that what happens in this new communication galaxy "affects the development of socialist culture, the security of information, and the stability of the state." Therefore, he argued, the Party "must strengthen efforts to develop and manage Internet culture and foster a good cyber environment" (Hu 2007).

China's rulers fear that the more citizens go online, the more they network with each other, the more the power monopoly of the Party is open to challenge. That is why the Party puts political pressure on national and foreign information technology companies (such as Chinese social networking providers Sina Weibo and Tencent, and American corporations such as Microsoft and Yahoo!) to censor, filter and control the growing flows of data exchanged on the web (MacKinnon, 2013). It is why Party officials insist that a key government priority is to establish a "clear and crisp" regulatory framework that improves "management of new network technologies and applications," especially through improved "emergency response systems" that handle "sudden incidents" and "maintain stability" (wéi hù wěn dìng) (China Copyright and Media, 2012; Creemers 2012). It is also why citizens who break the rules are subject to a wide assortment of informal and legal punishments, ranging from everyday harassment and hefty fines to multi-year incarceration.

The best-known government tool is the elaborate electronic surveillance system known officially as "the Golden Shield" (jīn dùn gōng chéng), but commonly referred to as the "Great Firewall of China" (fáng huǒ cháng chéng). It is a nation-wide electronic barrier that filters and controls information flows so that all data traffic in and out of China's internet passes through a limited number of check-points (gateways) controlled by ISPs, specially programmed network computers, or routers (Walton, 2001). The whole structure is sometimes officially likened to a system of rules and regulations for policing automobile traffic control, but the key difference is that Chinese users of digital media are often left in the dark about the routings and rules of the roads they take. Invisibility is the controlling norm. For instance, unless they have access to leaked memoranda, users never know whether or not the pages they are searching for are unavailable for technical reasons, or whether they have encountered government censorship as the Firewall's most distinctive feature is its secret lists of banned keywords and websites. Computer screens simply show a common error message (such as "site not found" wǎng zhàn zhǎo bú dào); sometimes, however, if users search for sensitive words using, for instance, Baidu.com, China's most popular web search engine, they might be greeted by a more revealing message that reads: "according to relevant laws, regulations and policies, the system doesn't show the content you are searching."

The official filtering system spots homonyms and synonyms and is continuously reviewed and upgraded, with new features such as the ability to detect, discover and block many (though not all) Virtual Private Network (VPN) providers, routinely used by citizens who want to access web services beyond the Firewall. An intriguing feature of the firewalling and filtering process is the way the Party censors keep everybody guessing. It's as if they want to mesmerise their subjects through "flexible censorship." Although some web pages (such as the *New York Times*) are permanently blocked, especially when they publish stories deemed too politically sensitive, the list of censored websites and keywords is not permanently fixed. Some sites are normally accessible, but blocked at more sensitive moments, as happened (in early 2013) to both the *Global Times* and the Guangzhou-based *Southern Weekend* after publishing an open letter criticising the Party's rewriting of the *Southern Weekend*'s new year's editorial, headed "China's Dream, the Dream of Constitutionalism." The Guangzhou newspaper's website was promptly shutdown, officially because its licence had expired; the open letter page on the *Global Times* website returned a "site not found" message; and such terms as "Southern" and "Weekend" connected to the incident were suddenly blacklisted. Under the Golden Shield, such measures are quite normal; constantly tweaked "flexible" controls that pre-determine what information citizens can download, read, publish or distribute are commonplace. The whole system frowns upon the anonymity of users. Regulations demand that users wishing to create a website must register with internet regulators in person, and present their ID. Real-name registration is a legal requirement for all internet users when uploading videos on online platforms. The same rule applies to all mobile application developers and all microblog and instant message tool users (China Copyright Media, 2014). The system of censorship naturally requires the cooperation of digital technology companies. Party documents emphasise the need to be permanently on the lookout for "any threat to the state's power, sovereignty, or the sustainable growth of the economy" (MacKinnon 2013, 36–37-139; "Race to the Bottom": Corporate Complicity in Chinese Internet Censorship, 2006, 12; China Copyright and Media, 2012). Foreign companies, such as Cisco Systems, the world's leading supplier of networking management and equipment, are caught up in this system; so, too, are companies involved in the building of China's cloud computing industry, such as Amazon, IBM and Microsoft.

[...]

Conclusions

All these initiatives, all the trends in the field of digital communications described in this article, serve as reminders that the whole story of digital media and politics in China is not straightforwardly reducible to matters of complex censorship mechanisms. There is much more beyond that. The trends reveal, in fact, how the technological revolution of the last two decades has forced Party leaders and officials to confront a new type of weakness: in a heavily networked society, where nothing is set in stone; there are no easy solutions to the Party's continuous struggle to avoid digital storms, to keep the status quo unchanged, and to produce and control public opinion. The core problem of the Communist Party's complex love-hate relationship with the internet is traceable to the distributed quality of its networks. Online networks are designed to disregard any single centre of power and to treat hierarchy as an obstacle to their smooth functioning. The philosophy underpinning networks is entirely at odds with the CCP's historical vision of its leadership role in Chinese society. The internet's structural resistance to top-down control injects a measure of uncertainty and "weakness" in the complex power/conflict dynamics between the Communist Party state and its citizens. "Weakness" here refers to the practical impossibility of any actor within this new galaxy of communication to exert complete control over a highly distributed network within the complex network of networks known as the internet. Awareness of this shared weakness is a powerful enabler of bold and irreverent new forms of resistance that signal just how different the internet is from traditional patterns of mediated domination. The tragic events in Tiananmen Square in 1989 taught the government of Beijing an important lesson: not only can media strengthen protests by stoking their momentum, but when protests are over the media are the repository of potentially dangerous collective memories.

> *"The further politicization of this issue comes, in large part, from the heavy lobbying that telecommunications companies like AT&T, Verizon and Comcast have been conducting."*

Regulations Are Prohibiting the Expansion of High-Speed Internet

Shane Burley

In the following viewpoint, Shane Burley argues that anti-net neutrality sentiments are based on the argument that those rules prohibit the expansion of high-speed internet and that many internet consumers are concerned that the current Republican-led FCC in 2017 may repeal multiple regulations that protect consumers, in favor of the interests of major telecommunications companies. If ISPs were able to sell the abilities to provide a "fast lane" to consumers able to pay for the service, Burley argues that it would stifle the ability for small businesses to grow in the current digital age, and small websites already in business today may have to shut down if they are unable to pay the predicted high costs. Burley is a writer and filmmaker based in Portland, Oregon.

As you read, consider the following questions:

1. Why do net neutrality proponents think that treating all websites the same is crucial for a free and open internet?
2. How would the repeal of net neutrality regulations negatively impact the future of media and journalism?
3. What are ways in which the foundational principles of net neutrality can be maintained if net neutrality regulations are repealed?

For many on the left, the string of appointments that have made up the president's new administration have been discussed as a horror show. While many have been sent reeling by major appointments like Jeff Sessions and Steve Bannon, they are eclipsing others that could have significant policy effects.

Trump's selection of Mark Jamison, a former lobbyist for the telecomm giant Sprint, and Jeffrey Eisenach, a consultant for Verizon, to the Federal Communications Commission has made many advocates of "net neutrality" nervous. The fear is that they may represent the interests of telecommunications companies, which have a vested interest in going after the "open Internet." As FCC chairman Tom Wheeler stepped down and Ajit Pai—a high-ranking Republican and a fierce critic of the net neutrality rule—replaced him, the rules that cemented net neutrality into current policy are likely to be threatened. This move has put the issue of net neutrality back on the forefront of social discussions, and with any changes to the current policies there could be a catastrophic shift in the culture of media and e-commerce.

Both detractors and advocates of net neutrality often note that we currently live in the "wild west" of the Internet. While major media and commercial corporations dominate traffic on the web, someone with an idea and a little web ingenuity can create a website that has equal access to users as major platforms like Google or Amazon. No website is privileged in access and the only difference in the speed of load times or the quality of service comes from the website themselves, not the Internet Service Providers, or ISPs. In many countries that have more restrictions on speech and information, ISPs in a given area can limit access to certain sites and search topics, or just allow certain websites to load more quickly.

Without net neutrality rules, which are a set of regulations that require ISPs to treat all websites the same, ISPs could create a paid "fast lane" for some websites that would allow them to have much faster load times and easier access. In a number of recent studies, these load times mean everything for websites struggling to compete. Milliseconds can change a purchasing decision from one company to a competitor and has a special effect on the use of video and streaming audio, where even a small reduction in speed makes load times unbearable.

If load speeds could essentially be purchased through an ISP determined "fast lane," then this could create a strong barrier to entry for small start-ups, new online retailers, and alternative and independent media sources. This could also have a devastating effect on American commerce, as the platforms would be stacked heavily in favor of massive companies—thereby lowering the opportunities for small businesses, which are still the largest type of employer in the country.

For journalists, this could lead to the shuttering of more news websites that will not be able to compete with these new rules. Meanwhile, the voices involved in civic discourse will further centralize into communications mega-corporations.

While companies like Google and Netflix have voiced opposition to this, they may end up getting in line with the new rules as a matter of business, essentially setting a tone of acceptance for the rest of the web.

As a new Republican administration gets comfortable in Washington, the issue of net neutrality is being newly politicized. Trump himself has tweeted that net neutrality is a top-down "power grab," a talking point that critics argue is disconnected from the actual issue. The further politicization of this issue comes, in large

INSUFFICIENT INFRASTRUCTURE

Did you pay for an expensive pay-per-view or streaming pass to watch the hyped-up boxing match between Floyd Mayweather and Conor McGregor, only to boil with rage as your access went down? You're far from alone. Numerous reports have revealed that servers across the US crashed or buckled under demand for the fight, creating outages serious enough that organizers delayed the fight to make sure people could tune in. Mayweather himself said that pay-per-view servers in California and Florida crashed, while Showtime and UFC failed to load, ran into login trouble and otherwise couldn't keep up with interest.

The pay-per-view issues at a minimum are known to have affected TV providers like Comcast, Atlantic Broadband and Frontier, although it's not clear how large the scope of the failures was at this stage.

Problems like this aren't completely unprecedented—Mayweather's fight against Manny Pacquiao created hiccups of its own. However, the sheer range of failures suggests that networks still haven't created infrastructures that can keep up with huge viewership spikes. At the same time, it also says something about how much sports viewing has changed in just a few years. You're now quite likely to hear people griping en masse about access to legal online streams where they might have resorted to bootleg streams or (gasp) conventional TV just a few years ago. And with networks like ESPN rushing to stream boxing to everyone, not just cable diehards, the importance of online access is only going to increase in the near future.

"Demand for Mayweather-McGregor Fight Crashed Pay-Per-View Servers," by Jon Fingas, Oath Tech Network Aol Tech, August 27, 2017.

part, from the heavy lobbying that telecommunications companies like AT&T, Verizon and Comcast have been conducting, amplifying the already dominant voices of communications mega-corporations that see net neutrality as meddling regulation.

While the money being thrown around by the telecommunications industry has been deafening, open Internet advocacy organizations are relying on the power of mass support to be the critical weapon. When the Stop Internet Privacy Act, or SOPA, was being debated, the entire country revolted. Many major Internet-based companies voiced their horror at the legislation—which would have increased the ability of law enforcement to go after digital file sharing—and participated in the American Censorship Day, a coalition effort of organizations and companies protesting against government intrusion into web access.

The Electronic Frontier Foundation, or EFF, an advocacy organization known for defending consumers and developers against government overreach in the digital landscape, was one of the organizations leading this charge. On January 18, 2012, some 75,000 websites went completely black in an effort to bring the Internet to a complete standstill. This bold action was heard clearly in Washington and resulted in those censorship bills being scrapped. As net neutrality heads back into Washington's crosshairs, the EFF is again taking a lead in confronting this possibility head on.

"[Abandoning net neutrality] would distort what we are used to, which is an open platform where we can go anywhere to something that looks more like cable television," said Ernesto Falcon, legislative council for the EFF.

Right now the FCC is the primary body where these rules could get changed, and it is this point that the EFF is staying focused on. This starts by making sure the voice of the people is sent directly to the FCC if those decisions begin to be reconsidered, making sure that the arguments made by the telecom industry are not considered without a challenge.

"Our effort is mainly to get the word out," Falcon said. "There were millions of people who already wrote to the FCC in favor of net neutrality … If politicians think that people want their Internet run by cable companies, they have another thing coming."

Their approach relies on the public commenting period that the FCC rules require. The EFF can then organize to flood the FCC with oppositional messages so that those voices in favor of Internet restriction will appear minuscule. If the net neutrality rules are then successfully repealed, the EFF will shift back into its legal role, challenging the FCC's decisions in the courts.

They have used this tactic to great effect before. After an action called "Occupy the FCC" began in May of 2014, which was a public encampment of multiple tents in front of the commission, the FCC's website was flooded by 3.7 million public comments supporting net neutrality. This voice of concern did not happen in a vacuum, as the Center for Media Justice organized a coalition of over a hundred organizations from a variety of backgrounds to confront the FCC and treat net neutrality as a social justice issue with an intersectional analysis. Rallies and protests targeting Comcast and Verizon were held across the country, uniting grassroots action with concerted and focused messaging about what was at stake if the Internet was consolidated by massive telecomm companies. This multifaceted campaign pushed Wheeler to establish the rules.

While the EFF has been fighting for digital rights for years, the enigmatic Fight for the Future project may be the best-known organization confronting the issue of net neutrality specifically. Starting in 2011, they created a model that uses tech tools to expand the voices of activists confronting encroachments on digital freedom. Not only were they key organizers in the world's largest digital protest around the SOPA, they were instrumental in having the net neutrality rules passed in the first place after they organized four million people to contact the FCC.

"[The] economic effects are huge," said Holmes Wilson, the co-director and co-founder of Fight for the Future. "If we lose net neutrality entire businesses will never happen."

Like the EFF, Fight for the Future is starting the battle at the FCC, since they see it as easier to challenge that body than confront Congress. "If we lose at the FCC, a new FCC can fix it. If we lose at Congress, every future FCC has their hands tied," Holmes said.

Legislation coming out of Congress would have a much more lasting effect on the issue, so if the FCC repeals net neutrality it would be much easier to correct than some type of binding legislation. Fight for the Future will be organizing a large contingent of stake-holders to contact senators and congress people who may have wavered on their commitment to an open Internet, focusing heavily on tech workers, small business owners, digital activists and those who would be intimately affected by a change in Internet oversight.

"We need to convince them, and if we can't convince them we need to pressure them," Holmes said.

This effort entails connecting with local groups to pressure legislators at a regional level, focusing on specific districts at a time. They are relying on an information campaign that will explain an issue that is rarely discussed and has been subject to misinformation and misunderstanding from large segments of the country.

The challenge for both organizations, and an increasing number of tech companies, journalists, and Internet advocates will be to replicate the success that earlier digital campaigns had. As Trump sets priorities for his new administration, telecommunications companies are continuing to flood money in to shift FCC policy to favor the largest media companies, putting an entire generation of Internet users at risk. While Trump has promised to pass through a number of controversial policies, organizations like the EFF and Fight for the Future are going to have to continue their public information campaign to explain why the issue of net neutrality is increasingly relevant.

The argument that telecommunications companies are now trying to make is that these regulations are prohibiting the expansion of high-speed Internet, and this strategy may have traction in an FCC built on the corporate-friendly attitude of the new president. Whether or not these types of counter-arguments are able to sway decisions will depend on how effectively these open Internet advocates are able to mobilize people, and to demonstrate how seemingly complex rules covering technology have intimate effects on the lives of everyday people.

> *"The world's largest democracy, with the second-most populous internet user base, India took a strong step forward in safeguarding Net Neutrality when it issued regulations in February 2016."*

Net Neutrality Matters for Human Rights

Access Now

In the following viewpoint, writers from Access Now detail actions taken to preserve net neutrality in multiple countries around the world, including India, which is banning "zero rating" practices and working toward binding regulations that prevent telecom companies from blocking or prioritizing internet content. Access Now argues that discriminatory services will not increases complete access to the internet, even if it is seen as viable for low-income users, because it is still censored and limited. Accesss Now is an international nonprofit, human rights, public policy, and advocacy group dedicated to an open and free internet.

As you read, consider the following questions:

1. Is it possible to maintain global net neutrality?
2. Why is the issue of "zero rating" at the core of international net neutrality discussions?
3. What are other countries around the world doing to preserve net neutrality?

If you're reading this, you've probably heard the internet is the first technology allowing anyone to express themselves on a global stage, without first asking permission from a company or government. But this is only true when we prevent internet service providers (ISPs) from abusing their control of internet access to lock out any new businesses or ideas they find threatening.

The only way to maintain global internet freedom is to have global Net Neutrality, and the only way to have global Net Neutrality is to enact a quilt of enforceable policies that cover every one of the world's more than 10,000 ISPs.

Access Now has been working towards global Net Neutrality since we were founded in 2009, and many of our international partners have been in the fight for even longer. We have helped secure Net Neutrality for hundreds of millions of people, but we still have a long way to go.

Over the past three years, we have seen hard-won victories on Net Neutrality come under threat. Activists in advanced economies are struggling to communicate the importance of Net Neutrality for free expression, innovation, and competition, in some cases to audiences that are increasingly anti-regulation. Many in developing countries are facing down critics who argue that non-neutral internet access somehow functions as an "on-ramp" for the free and open internet (even as new research bolsters the evidence that it does not).

Today in the US, activists are submitting final comments in a proceeding before the US Federal Communications Commission (FCC) that threatens to roll back the historic Open Internet Rules of 2014. At the same time, in India, which early last year [2016] took the laudable step of banning the controversial practice of "zero rating," the Telecom Regulatory Authority of India (TRAI) has just concluded the last of its "open house" discussions in its consultation on Net Neutrality, which is meant to put in place rules to prevent technical discrimination by gatekeeping telecom companies, such as blocking, throttling, or prioritization.

Below we tour three global "hot spots" in the struggle for Net Neutrality, principles that are essential for free expression in the digital age. We hope that wherever you hail from, if you value a free and open internet, you will get involved.

Net Neutrality in India: Closer to the Finish Line

Over this summer and monsoon, Indians have eagerly awaited progress on establishing a comprehensive set of rules on Net Neutrality, a step that has been pending since 2015. The world's largest democracy, with the second-most populous internet user base, India took a strong step forward in safeguarding Net Neutrality when it issued regulations in February 2016 to ban zero rating, the practice wherein ISPs give preferential treatment to selected services or applications, influencing the user experience and distorting competition.

Only a year before issuing those regulations, the TRAI had published a consultation paper on licensing internet services and applications (under the garb of troubling "OTT" regulation), and had been skeptical of protecting Net Neutrality. This remarkable turn-around was a product of unprecedented public mobilization in favor of protecting a free and open internet. No fewer than 1.2 million Indians wrote to the TRAI asking them to #SaveTheInternet and this triggered widespread public support for action to legally protect Net Neutrality.

Since then, however, the regulatory process has been running at a slow, deliberative pace. The TRAI acted on earlier promises to advance its Net Neutrality regulatory consultative process by first issuing a pre-consultation paper on the topic in May 2016 and finally publishing the full consultation paper in January 2017. Comments and counter-comments to this consultation concluded officially in April 2017, and beginning in mid-summer, the TRAI has been organizing in-person open house discussion meetings, hosted across India's financial, tech, and political hub cities of Mumbai, Bengaluru, and Delhi.

Telecom industry lobbyists have been seeking to sway the TRAI away from the demand by Indian citizens for clear, impactful Net Neutrality rules, as well as lobbying to roll back TRAI's landmark February 2016 differential data pricing rules. With the conclusion of the last open house discussion in Delhi today, TRAI Chairman R.S. Sharma has indicated that it is seeking to deliver an outcome towards the end of September.

At stake here is ensuring that at the end of the process, there are clear, binding regulations to prevent telecom companies from unjustly blocking, throttling, or prioritizing internet content to favor their interests, rather than serving those of their current users and the next billion people coming online to the internet.

Net Neutrality in Europe: The Watchers of the Law

In Brussels, lawmakers adopted rules to implement Net Neutrality in October 2015. Since then, BEREC—the E.U. regulators—has further clarified the rules, and this has served largely to reinforce users' rights. Yet some uncertainties remain, in particular on the issue of zero rating. BEREC is currently consulting the public to establish clear technical criteria to monitor implementation of Net Neutrality rules across all member states.

In short, this means that the situation in the E.U. is largely positive, but not quite perfect. Back in 2016, BEREC decided, unwisely in our view, not to ban zero rating altogether. BEREC settled upon a case by case approach, wherein telecoms regulators assess whether each zero rating offer complies with Net Neutrality rules. This has already led to a foreseeable—and harmful—

patchwork of interpretation by telcos. This is an issue that must be addressed to stop this form of abuse from taking root in the E.U. market and jeopardizing Net Neutrality in Europe.

Net Neutrality in the United States: Winter Is Coming

The fight for Net Neutrality is incredibly contentious in the US, where the FCC, now under the control of Chairman Ajit Pai, seems committed to rolling back the rules passed in 2014. The US had previously set a positive example for the rest of the world when it passed bright line rules to protect Net Neutrality. These rules are at now risk.

Access Now and about 22 million others submitted comments to the FCC on its new rollback proposal; in our comment we push not only to maintain but also to strengthen the 2014 rules. Today the FCC closes a second round of "reply comments" on Chairman Pai's plan and we're working with partners and allies to make sure they hear the demands from people in the US and around the world.

Global Warning: Zero Rating Is on the Rise

The issue of zero rating has been at the core of Net Neutrality discussions across the globe, and it's not going away anytime soon. Through these discriminatory practices, internet users are offered free or prioritized access to some, but not all, of the internet, resulting in unequal access. All around the world, telecoms and tech companies are pushing zero-rated services, sometimes marketing them as a first gateway to get more people online. While giving more people access to the free and open internet is a laudable goal, zero rating has largely failed to deliver on that promise. Instead, it has increased the risks for human rights violations.

Zero rating limits the number of platforms and websites through which we can easily communicate and access information. It gives operators incentives to scrutinize our data traffic in order to discover which content, apps, and services are the most popular, and then to strike deals for prioritization. This in turn makes surveillance and censorship much easier, as the data flows through only a limited number of easily identifiable channels. Research into the use of zero rating offers shows that services like Facebook's "Free Basics" are a pathway to consolidate market power and that a different, more intrusive, data policy applies when using social media through these services. Worryingly, a study from GSMA showed that people often conflate Facebook with the internet.

A more recent study by Global Voices—funded through Access Now Grants—provides additional evidence that zero-rated programs like Free Basics do not bring new users online, but instead accomplish what can be described as "digital colonialism." Deploying discriminatory services is not the right way to increase access to the internet, since it also increases the risks for human rights. Instead, those seeking to expand access to the internet should invest in, or create incentives for investing in, infrastructure. That way, we ensure that everyone can benefit from the free and open internet, which can act both as a vehicle for the enjoyment of human rights and a spur to innovation and development globally (helping us to reach the U.N. Sustainable Development Goals).

> "Under the current rules, the FCC
> can intervene to prevent a major
> ISP with a vast network from
> leveraging its massive network size
> in an anti-competitive way to harm
> other networks."

Small ISPs Want Net Neutrality

Ernesto Falcon

In the following viewpoint, Ernesto Falcon argues that FCC chair Ajit Pai's insistence that small ISPs are impacted negatively by the 2015 Open Internet Order is inconsistent. Falcon also establishes that, while there have been multiple anti–net neutrality arguments made in attempt to support small ISPs, they have been debunked, and small ISPs prefer the net neutrality regulations to remain in place so that major market powers like Comcast, AT&T, and Verizon are reined in. Falcon is a legislative counsel at the Electronic Frontier Foundation, with a primary focus on intellectual property and open internet issues.

"More than 40 ISPs Across the Country Tell Chairman Pai to Not Repeal Network Neutrality and Maintain Title II Enforcement," by Ernesto Falcon, Electronic Frontier Foundation, June 27, 2017. https://www.eff.org/deeplinks/2017/06/isps-across-country-tell-chairman-pai-not-repeal-network-neutrality. Licensed under CC BY 3.0 US.

As you read, consider the following questions:

1. Per the viewpoint, how does Title II of the Communications Act promote competition in broadband access?
2. What needs to be done to further ensure that ISPs know their legal obligations regarding their consumer data?
3. How does Section 251 of the Communications Act protect consumer interests?

One excuse FCC Chairman Ajit Pai regularly offers to explain his effort to gut net neutrality protections is the claim that open Internet rules have harmed ISPs, especially small ones. During a speech earlier this year, he stressed that 22 small ISPs told him that the 2015 Open Internet Order hurt their ability to invest and deploy.

In reality, though, many more ISPs feel very differently. Today, more than 40 ISPs told the FCC that they have had no problem with the Open Internet Order and that it hasn't hurt their ability to develop and expand their networks. What is more, that they want the FCC to do its job and address the problem Congress created when it repealed the broadband privacy rules in March.

Why These ISPs Like Title II

The 2015 Order famously outlined clear net neutrality rules. But those rules only passed muster because the Order also explicitly classified broadband service as a "common carrier" service, regulated by Title II of the Communications Act, rather than an "information service" regulated by Title I of the same Act. And that classification has several corollary effects, because Title II isn't just about net neutrality. It is also meant to curtail the anti-competitive conduct from incumbent monopolists like Comcast, AT&T, and Verizon. In essence, as common carriers, they are not able to use their power to control the Internet experience, and they are not able to directly harm their competitors in the broadband market.

That's why these small ISPs are worried. Chairman Pai wants to reverse the 2015 decision to reclassify broadband as a "common carrier" service, thereby eliminating the protections Title II offers. If he succeeds, not only are Section 201 and Section 202—the core provisions that support network neutrality—on the chopping block, but also a whole host of other active provisions that protect competition in the broadband market. Small wonder the big cable and telephone lobbies are happy to pay lip service to net neutrality—so long as the actual rules aren't based on Title II.

To start, Section 251 of the Communications Act requires broadband providers to "interconnect" with other broadband providers and related market players in order to prevent the possibility of a large player (back in the day that was AT&T) from denying access to the network by simply denying physical connectivity. While more clarity is needed from the FCC on how it intends to manage interconnection disputes, it was clear that the FCC had to play a role as problems began to arise. We saw this play out most notably with Netflix traffic, whether it is Comcast disputing the delivery of Comcast customer requested traffic to their homes, to the direct dispute between Comcast and Netflix before the 2015 FCC Order. Under the current rules, the FCC can intervene to prevent a major ISP with a vast network from leveraging its massive network size in an anti-competitive way to harm other networks. That oversight vanishes if Chairman Pai reclassifies broadband as an "information service," which undoubtedly Comcast would appreciate.

Another example of how Title II of the Communications Act promotes competition in broadband access is the relatively unknown issue of pole attachment rights under Section 224 of the Communications Act. Today, that section ensures that every broadband provider has the legal right to gain access to many of the poles that run along our roads. These poles, and other rights of way infrastructure, are the route that any broadband company must travel in order to get to your home or business. Google

Fiber's deployment ran into snags in Austin, Texas when those poles were owned by AT&T, because the surest way to prevent competition is to just physically prevent their entry into your market. If a company the size of Google could be stifled without the law supporting them, what hope does a smaller ISP have in entering into a market where the incumbent broadband provider owns the poles that are a necessary component to deploying the network? The FCC Chairman's plan fundamentally ignores this problem and offers no clear solution to competitors. An incumbent broadband provider that owns a lot of the poles is going to have no federal legal obligation to share that access at fair market rates if broadband is no longer a common carrier service.

Lastly, Section 222 ensures that broadband users have a legal right to privacy when we use broadband communications. It has already taken a beating, thanks to Congress' misguided decision to repeal the FCC's rules that had been based on Section 222, but the section itself is still the law today. The problem now is that ISPs do not know their legal obligations with consumer data and how they are supposed to operate without more FCC guidance. Undoubtedly, the large cable and telephone companies that spent millions to lobby Congress to repeal the rules intend to profit from the vast treasure trove of personal data that runs over their networks. But ISPs opposed to Chairman Pai's plan are not looking to make more money off of their customers by selling their personal data without permission. Almost all of them were strongly opposed to Congress repealing the privacy rules. None of them got into the business of providing access to the Internet so they could snoop on the activities of their customers. However, Chairman Pai's plan would outright remove the Section 222 privacy obligations for all broadband companies and as a result there would be absolutely no way to have broadband privacy rules absent a new law. In essence, Chairman Pai's plan would be the nail in the coffin for broadband privacy that Congress started with its privacy repeal earlier this year.

What Is the FCC Plan for Smaller Competitors in the Broadband Market?

There is no plan. We have no alternative body of law beyond the Communications Act and the provisions of Title II to address the competition issues listed above. Antitrust is generally not a viable option as well. That is why Pai's plan is not about improving the investment opportunities for all broadband providers (a claim that has been thoroughly debunked twice now and now outright refuted by more than 40 ISPs themselves). Instead, it is a plan to radically enhance the market power of Comcast, AT&T, and Verizon in a way that no previous FCC Chair (both Republican and Democrat) ever entertained.

These ISPs are taking a stand for network neutrality because they know Chairman Pai's plan will hurt them as well as their subscribers. Contact the FCC and Congress today to tell them to oppose Chairman Pai's plan to empower major cable and telephone companies.

> *"Another lever that states and malicious actors often reach for when seeking to censor legitimate voices is through denial-of-service attacks."*

Censoring Content Is Counter to Net Neutrality

Jeremy Malcolm, Cindy Cohn, and Danny O'Brien

In the following viewpoint, Jeremy Malcolm, Cindy Cohn, and Danny O'Brien comment on actions taken by some web-based companies to refuse service to the neo-Nazi website the Daily Stormer. While the move was favored on the public level, the authors argue that it sets a potentially problematic precedent regarding how companies choose to censor the content on the internet. The writers end the viewpoint with a recommendation that companies adhere to a clear and transparent process regarding content they manage. Jeremy Malcolm, Cindy Cohn, and Danny O'Brien all work for the Electronic Frontier Foundation.

As you read, consider the following questions:

1. What are the potential ramifications of managing the protections of free speech on the internet?
2. Why is the domain name system a key part of the technical underbelly of the internet?
3. What are the Manila Principles?

In the wake of Charlottesville, both GoDaddy and Google have refused to manage the domain registration for the Daily Stormer, a neo-Nazi website that, in the words of the Southern Poverty Law Center, is "dedicated to spreading anti-Semitism, neo-Nazism, and white nationalism." Subsequently Cloudflare, whose service was used to protect the site from denial-of-service attacks, has also dropped them as a customer, with a telling quote from Cloudflare's CEO: "Literally, I woke up in a bad mood and decided someone shouldn't be allowed on the Internet. No one should have that power."

We agree. Even for free speech advocates, this situation is deeply fraught with emotional, logistical, and legal twists and turns. All fair-minded people must stand against the hateful violence and aggression that seems to be growing across our country. But we must also recognize that on the Internet, any tactic used now to silence neo-Nazis will soon be used against others, including people whose opinions we agree with. Those on the left face calls to characterize the Black Lives Matter movement as a hate group. In the Civil Rights Era cases that formed the basis of today's protections of freedom of speech, the NAACP's voice was the one attacked.

Protecting free speech is not something we do because we agree with all of the speech that gets protected. We do it because we believe that no one—not the government and not private commercial enterprises—should decide who gets to speak and who doesn't.

What Happened?

Earlier this week, following complaints about a vitriolic and abusive Daily Stormer article on Heather Heyer—the woman killed when a white nationalist drove a car into a crowd of anti-racism demonstrators—GoDaddy told the site's owners that they had 24 hours to leave their service. Daily Stormer subsequently moved their domain to Google's domain management service. Within hours Google announced that it too was refusing Daily Stormer as a customer. Google also placed the dailystormer.com domain on "Client Hold," which means that Daily Stormer's owner cannot activate, use or move the domain to another service. It's unclear whether this is for a limited amount of time, or whether Google has decided to effectively take ownership of the dailystormer.com domain permanently. Cloudflare, whose service was used to protect the site from denial-of-service attacks, subsequently dropped them as a customer.

We at EFF defend the right of anyone to choose what speech they provide online; platforms have a First Amendment right to decide what speech does and does not appear on their platforms. That's what laws like CDA 230 in the United States enable and protect.

But we strongly believe that what GoDaddy, Google, and Cloudflare did here was dangerous. That's because, even when the facts are the most vile, we must remain vigilant when platforms exercise these rights. Because Internet intermediaries, especially those with few competitors, control so much online speech, the consequences of their decisions have far-reaching impacts on speech around the world. And at EFF we see the consequences first hand: every time a company throws a vile neo-Nazi site off the Net, thousands of less visible decisions are made by companies with little oversight or transparency. Precedents being set now can shift the justice of those removals. Here's what companies and individuals should watch for in these troubling times.

Content Removal at the Very Top of the Internet

Domain registrars are one of many types of companies in the chain of online content distribution—the Internet intermediaries positioned between the writer or poster of speech and the reader of that speech. Other intermediaries include the ISP that delivers a website's content to end users, the certificate authority (such as Let's Encrypt) that issues an SSL certificate to the website, the content delivery network that optimizes the availability and performance of the website, the web hosting company that provides server space for the website, and even communications platforms—such as email providers and social media companies—that allow the website's URLs to be easily shared.

The domain name system is a key part of the Internet's technical underpinnings, which are enabled by an often-fragile consensus among many systems and operators. Using that system to edit speech, based on potentially conflicting opinions about what can be spoken on the Internet, risks shattering that consensus. Domain suspension is a blunt instrument: suspending the domain name of a website or Internet service makes everything hosted there difficult or impossible to access. The risk of blocking speech that wasn't targeted is very high.

Domain name companies also have little claim to be publishers, or speakers in their own right, with respect to the contents of websites. Like the suppliers of ink or electrical power to a pamphleteer, the companies that sponsor domain name registrations have no direct connection to Internet content. Domain name registrars have even less connection to speech than a conduit provider such as an ISP, as the contents of a website or service never touch the registrar's systems. Registrars' interests as speakers under the First Amendment are minimal.

If the entities that run the domain name system started choosing who could access or add to them based on political considerations, we might well face a world where every government and powerful body would see itself as an equal or more legitimate invoker of that power. That makes the domain name system unsuitable as a mechanism for taking down specific illegal content as the law sometimes requires, and a perennially attractive central location for nation-states and others to exercise much broader takedown powers.

Another lever that states and malicious actors often reach for when seeking to censor legitimate voices is through denial-of-service attacks. States and criminals alike use this to silence voices, and the Net's defenses against such actions are not well-developed. Services like Cloudflare can protect against these attacks, but not if they also face direct pressure from governments and other actors to pick and choose their clients. Content delivery networks are not wired into the infrastructure of the Net in the way that the domain name system is, but at this point, they may as well be.

These are parts of the Net that are most sensitive to pervasive censorship: they are free speech's weakest links. It's the reason why millions of net neutrality advocates are concerned about ISPs censoring their feeds. Or why, when the handful of global payment processors unite to block certain websites (like Wikileaks) worldwide, we should be concerned. These weak links are both the most tempting, and most egregiously damaging places, to filter the Net.

The firmest, most consistent, defense these potential weak links can take is to simply decline all attempts to use them as a control point. They can act to defend their role as a conduit, rather than a publisher. And just as law and custom developed a norm that we might sue a publisher for defamation, but not the owner of a printing press, or newspaper vendor, we are slowly developing norms about who should take responsibility for content online. Companies that manage domain names, including GoDaddy and Google, should draw a hard line: they should not suspend or impair domain names based on the expressive content of websites or services.

Have a Process, Don't Act on the Headlines

Other elements of the Net risk less when they are selective about who they host. But even for hosts, there's always a risk that others—including governments—will use the opaqueness of the takedown process to silence legitimate voices. For any content hosts that do reject content as part of the enforcement of their terms of service, or are pressured by states to secretly censor, we have long recommended that they implement procedural protections to mitigate mistakes—specifically, the Manila Principles on Intermediary Liability. The principles state, in part:

- Before any content is restricted on the basis of an order or a request, the intermediary and the user content provider must be provided an effective right to be heard except in exceptional circumstances, in which case a post facto review of the order and its implementation must take place as soon as practicable.
- Intermediaries should provide user content providers with mechanisms to review decisions to restrict content in violation of the intermediary's content restriction policies.
- Intermediaries should publish their content restriction policies online, in clear language and accessible formats, and keep them updated as they evolve, and notify users of changes when applicable.

These are methods that protect us all against overbroad or arbitrary takedowns. It's notable that in GoDaddy and Google's eagerness to swiftly distance themselves from American neo-Nazis, no process was followed; CloudFlare's Prince also admitted that the decision was "not CloudFlare's policy." Policies give guidance as to what we might expect, and an opportunity to see justice is done. We should think carefully before throwing them away.

It might seem unlikely now that Internet companies would turn against sites supporting racial justice or other controversial issues. But if there is a single reason why so many individuals and companies are acting together now to unite against neo-Nazis, it is because a future that seemed unlikely a few years ago—where white nationalists and Nazis have significant power and influence in our society—now seems possible. We would be making a mistake if we assumed that these sorts of censorship decisions would never turn against causes we love.

Part of the work for all of us now is to push back against such dangerous decisions with our own voices and actions. Another part of our work must be to seek to shore up the weakest parts of the Internet's infrastructure so it cannot be easily toppled if matters take a turn for the (even) worse. These actions are not in opposition; they are to the same ends.

We can—and we must—do both.

> *"What the US decides will determine whether US leadership on the internet remains strong, or whether it will cede ground to other countries willing to protect their citizens."*

The United States Is No Longer a Leader in Online Consumer Protection

Sascha Meinrath and Nathalia Foditsch

In the following viewpoint, Sascha Meinrath and Nathalia Foditsch argue that the United States is both a trailblazer and pulling up the rear when it comes to an open internet. The authors present historical examples of discriminatory practices exhibited by ISPs prior to the 2015 Open Internet Order. They make the case that if the United States goes backward, other countries might step in to become leaders in consumer protection. Meinrath is the Palmer Chair in Telecommunications at Penn State and director of X-Lab, an innovative think tank focusing on the intersection of vanguard technologies and public policy. Foditsch is a Brazilian attorney focused on communications policy and regulation.

As you read, consider the following questions:

1. Which company blocked access to Skype and FaceTime in 2009?
2. What is the consumer protection like in Europe, as of 2017?
3. How is India different from the United States in terms of net neutrality?

The internet may be an international system of interconnecting networks sharing a rough global consensus about the technical details of communicating through them—but each country manages its own internet environment independently. As the US debate about the role of government in overseeing and regulating the internet continues, it's worth looking at how other countries handle the issue.

Our research and advocacy on internet regulation in the US and other countries offers us a unique historical and global perspective on the Federal Communications Commission's December 2017 decision to deregulate the internet in the US. The principle of an open internet, often called "net neutrality," is one of consumer protection. It is based on the idea that everyone—users and content providers alike—should be able to freely spread their own views, and consumers can choose what services to use and what content to consume. Network neutrality ensures that no one—not the government, nor corporations—is allowed to censor speech or interfere with content, services or applications.

As the US continues to debate whether to embrace internet freedom, the world is doing so already, with many countries imposing even stronger rules than the ones the FCC did away with.

The US as Trailblazer and Laggard

Before 2015, many internet businesses in the US discriminated against or blocked customers from particular legal uses of the internet. In 2007 Comcast illegally blocked its customers from sharing files between themselves. In 2009, AT&T blocked access to Skype and FaceTime apps on its network. In 2011, MetroPCS blocked its customers from streaming Netflix and all other streaming video except YouTube (possibly due to a secretly negotiated deal). In 2012, Verizon disabled apps that let customers connect computers to their mobile data service. There were many other violations of the principle of net neutrality, too.

Customers and regulators tried to control these discriminatory practices over many years of public deliberation and multiple court cases. In 2015, under the Obama administration, the FCC finalized the Open Internet Order, a set of rules barring internet service providers from speeding up or slowing down traffic based on its content or whether the companies posting it had paid extra to the company delivering the data. It was far from perfect—but nonetheless a giant leap forward.

In early 2017, after his inauguration, President Trump appointed Ajit Pai, a former Verizon lawyer, as the FCC chairman. Pai, an Obama appointee to the FCC who had voted against the Open Internet Order in 2015, has moved rapidly to undo it. He and some other comentators believe that customers will get better service from a less-regulated market, ignoring that the rules only emerged in the wake of problems and consumer complaints.

Pai's proposal has been criticized by former FCC Chairman Tom Wheeler as "a shameful sham and sellout" to big telecommunications companies. A who's-who list of the people who invented the technologies and systems underlying the internet denounced Pai's policy as "based on a flawed and factually inaccurate understanding of internet technology."

Other countries are facing similar dilemmas about how to deal with today's digital realities, and are slowly and individually contributing to a patchwork of laws that differ from country to country. But many highly industrialized and rapidly developing countries share a general consensus that regulations ensuring an open internet are good for consumers and for civil society.

Opening the Internet Brazilian Style

Brazil's Civil Rights Framework for the Internet, enacted in 2014 and further refined in 2016, only allows internet service companies to prioritize certain types of traffic for technical reasons—such as overloaded networking capacity—or to allow network use by emergency services.

Yet, the country has been reluctant to enforce these rules and hold violators to account. Much like in the US, there is increasing concern that industry power has overwhelmed government regulatory agencies. Some of the largest telecommunications companies have been providing their mobile internet customers with preferential access to content on sites and services owned by business partners. Many Brazilian consumer rights groups are particularly alarmed because the companies receiving this privileged treatment are all large foreign corporations, including Facebook, WhatsApp, Twitter and music-streaming service Deezer (the only non-US company).

In addition, there are proposals in the works that would grant tens of millions of dollars in publicly owned telecommunications infrastructure to private companies for free. Brazilian internet freedom is further at risk because the country's telecommunications companies are planning to insist that its regulators align with the weakened US rules.

Active Enforcement in Europe

The European Union approved strong rules in 2015, requiring companies that provide internet access to handle all traffic equally, leaving flexibility to restrict traffic when network equipment was operating at its maximum capacity. EU rules also allow traffic restrictions to protect network security and handle emergency situations.

In 2016, European Union electronic communications regulators detailed potential problems in agreements between telecommunications companies and content providers. And they explained that quality of service could vary, but no specific applications should be discriminated against.

In 2017, they highlighted the importance of Europe's emphasis on proactively monitoring compliance with net neutrality rules, rather than waiting for violations to happen before reacting. This gives European residents much stronger consumer protection than exists in the US.

India Takes a Stand

India has taken similarly strong steps. In 2016, the Telecom Regulatory Authority of India approved rules stating that "no service provider shall offer or charge discriminatory tariffs for data services on the basis of content." In November 2017, the agency also issued "recommendations on net neutrality," laying out rules of the road for internet service providers that incorporate substantial protections against content and application discrimination.

Indian regulators are looking to balance consumer and corporate priorities in areas such as security, privacy and ownership of data. Moreover, they are considering adopting regulations to spur competition in mobile data services.

Most importantly, Indian regulators make very clear that companies providing internet service should not do anything "that has the effect of discriminatory treatment based on content, sender or receiver, protocols or user equipment." This puts openness at the core of internet service, the sort of clear consumer protection that public interest advocates and academics have called for.

The US Isn't an Island

The US internet industry is a powerful global force, with billions of users of its websites and online services all around the world. Further, the US government has traditionally been a leader in developing policies that balance free speech, consumer protection and other civil rights with strong opportunities for research and business innovation—but this too is now in decline.

Net neutrality protections might not be so necessary if the broadband market were more competitive. But 29 percent of Americans have no options for getting high-speed wired internet service at home. Another 47 percent have just one choice—and 20 percent have just two.

The telecommunications industry continues to consolidate—though the US Department of Justice is trying to block the pending AT&T-Time Warner merger. In this market with few providers, and many companies seeking profits by promoting their own content via their own networks, net neutrality protections will only become more important—not less so.

Lastly, legally speaking, policy and regulatory decisions made in the US don't hold any direct power in other countries. However, domestic rules about the internet will indeed affect the global conversation around net neutrality. What the US decides, through the FCC, the courts and potentially even through Congress, will determine whether US leadership on the internet remains strong, or whether it will cede ground to other countries willing to protect their citizens.

Periodical and Internet Sources Bibliography

The following articles have been selected to supplement the diverse views presented in this chapter.

Liz Alderman and Amie Tsang, "Net Neutrality's Holes in Europe May Offer Peek at Future in U.S.," *New York Times*, December 10, 2017. https://www.nytimes.com/2017/12/10/business/net -neutrality-europe-fcc.html.

American Civil Liberties Union, "ACLU Comment on FCC Plan to End Net Neutrality," November 21, 2017. https://www.aclu.org /news/aclu-comment-fcc-plan-end-net-neutrality.

American Civil Liberties Union, "Network Neutrality 101: Why the Government Must Act to Preserve the Free and Open Internet," October 2010. https://www.aclu.org/report/network-neutrality -101-why-government-must-act-preserve-free-and-open -internet.

Aaron Bandler, "7 Reasons Net Neutrality Is Idiotic," Daily Wire, July 14, 2017. https://www.dailywire.com/news/18613/7-reasons-net -neutrality-idiotic-aaron-bandler.

Ananya Bhattacharya, "India Is Upholding an Open Internet as the US Moves to Dismantle Net Neutrality," Quartz India, November 29, 2017. https://qz.com/1140558/net-neutrality-indias-trai-is -upholding-an-open-internet-as-the-fcc-moves-to-dismantle-it -in-the-us/.

James Gattuso, "Net Neutrality Rules: Still a Threat to Internet Freedom," Heritage, February 12, 2014. http://www.heritage.org /government-regulation/report/net-neutrality-rules-still-threat -internet-freedom.

Adrianne Jeffries, "The Daily Stormer Just Lost Its New .cat Domain," Outline, October 6, 2017. https://theoutline.com/post/2376/the -daily-stormer-just-lost-its-new-cat-domain.

Andrei Khalip and Agnieszka Flak, "False Paradise? EU Is No Haven of Net Neutrality, Say Critics," Reuters, December 15, 2017. https://www.reuters.com/article/us-usa-internet-eu-analysis /false-paradise-eu-is-no-haven-of-net-neutrality-say-critics -idUSKBN1E92SC.

Cheang Ming and Saheli Roy Choudhury, "China Has Launched Another Crackdown on the Internet—but It's Different This

Time," CNBC, October 26, 2017. https://www.cnbc.com /2017/10/26/china-internet-censorship-new-crackdowns-and -rules-are-here-to-stay.html.

Paul Mozur, "Inside China's Big Tech Conference, New Ways to Track Citizens," *New York Times*, December 5, 2017. https://www .nytimes.com/2017/12/05/business/china-internet-conference- wuzhen.html?rref=collection%2Ftimestopic%2FInternet%20 Censorship%20in%20China&action=click&contentCollection =world&region=stream&module=stream_unit&version =latest&contentPlacement=1&pgtype=collection.

Jason Oxman, "The FCC and the Unregulation of the Internet," Counsel for Advanced Communications Office of Plans and Policy, July 1999. https://transition.fcc.gov/Bureaus/OPP /working_papers/oppwp31.pdf.

Prasanto K. Roy, "India Net Neutrality Rules Could Be World's Strongest," BBC, November 30, 2017. http://www.bbc.com/news /world-asia-india-42162979.

Maryam Saleh and Ryan Grimm, "Neo-Nazi Website the Daily Stormer Is Now Being Hosted on an Island with Mostly Black Residents," *Intercept*, October 27, 2017. https://theintercept .com/2017/10/27/daily-stormer-anguilla-web-domain/.

Sebastien Soriano, "Europe Has a Message for Americans on Net Neutrality," *Slate*, December 12, 2017. http://www.slate.com /articles/technology/future_tense/2017/12/france_s_top _internet_regulator_s_bastien_soriano_has_a_message_for _americans.html.

Josh Steimle, "Am I the Only Techie Against Net Neutrality?," *Forbes*, May 14, 2014. https://www.forbes.com/sites/joshsteimle /2014/05/14/am-i-the-only-techie-against-net-neutrality /#58a2ee3770d5.

Alan Wolk, "The Repeal of Net Neutrality Is a Bad Thing (but Not for the Reasons You Think)," *Forbes*, November 30, 2017. https:// www.forbes.com/sites/alanwolk/2017/11/30/the-repeal-of -net-neutrality-is-a-bad-thing-but-not-for-the-reasons-you -think/#16632a5d65be.

For Further Discussion

Chapter 1

1. April Glaser uses multiple examples of telecommunications companies censoring content on the internet. How would that impact the principles of net neutrality, and what policies should be implemented to stop that from happening in the future?
2. Per Chinelo Nkechi Ikem's commentary on class issues concerning net neutrality, what are ways in which lower-income communities can access the internet, and why are they not enough to thoroughly prove that the internet is available to all?
3. Considering the commentaries provided in Kerry Sheehan's viewpoint, has the argument for or against net neutrality in the United States truly fallen on party lines? Explain why or why not.

Chapter 2

1. Justin Fox wrote about net neutrality before the 2015 decision, which has since been overturned. What does this tell you about net neutrality? How do you think users and ISPs will respond to future changes to net neutrality rulings?
2. Daniel Lyons uses the Bell Telephone Company monopoly to explain why classifying broadband communications under Title II negatively impacts consumers. Are his arguments sound? Why or why not?
3. Drew Armstrong uses claims from the FTC that FCC intervention in net neutrality regulation is unnecessary. Does the FTC do enough to protect consumers through antitrust regulation? Why or why not?

Chapter 3

1. Maureen K. Ohlhausen explains the history of the FCC's attempts to curtail ISP misconduct. Explain why questions regarding its regulatory authority make it difficult for the FCC to pursue these cases.

2. Using the information in Lori McGlinchey's viewpoint, explain the benefits of net neutrality from a social point of view and the grassroots efforts involved in its preservation.

3. Alina Selukh points out that Congress may ultimately be the body that settles the net neutrality debate. What are the benefits and drawbacks to partisan and bipartisan federal regulations?

Chapter 4

1. Shane Burley addresses the potential problems for journalists if load speeds can be purchased through a fast lane. How would that impact the information we receive?

2. Jeremy Malcolm, Cindy Cohn, and Danny O'Brien point out the potential problems that come with outright censoring of websites, like what happened to the Daily Stormer. While free speech is protected under the US Constitution, is hate speech? Additionally, what can legally be done to curtail hate speech online?

Organizations to Contact

The editors have compiled the following list of organizations concerned with the issues debated in this book. The descriptions are derived from materials provided by the organizations. All have publications or information available for interested readers. The list was compiled on the date of publication of the present volume; the information provided here may change. Be aware that many organizations take several weeks or longer to respond to inquiries, so allow as much time as possible.

Access Now

PO Box 20429, Greeley Square Station, 4 E. Twenty-Seventh St., New York, NY 10001-9998
(888) 414-0100
email: info@accessnow.com
website: www.accessnow.org

Access Now defends and extends the digital rights of users at risk around the world. By combining innovative policy, global advocacy, and direct technical support, we fight for open and secure communications for all.

American Civil Liberties Union (ACLU)

125 Broad St., 18th Floor, New York, NY 10004
(212) 549-2500
website: www.aclu.org

For nearly one hundred years, the ACLU has been our nation's guardian of liberty, working in courts, legislatures, and communities to defend and preserve the individual rights and liberties that the Constitution and the laws of the United States guarantee everyone in this country.

American Enterprise Institute

1789 Massachusetts Ave. NW, Washington, DC 20036
(202) 862-5800
email: mediaservices@aei.org
website: www.aei.org

The American Enterprise Institute is a public policy think tank dedicated to defending human dignity, expanding human potential, and building a freer and safer world. The work of the group's scholars and staff advances ideas rooted in their belief in democracy, free enterprise, American strength and global leadership, solidarity with those at the periphery of our society, and a pluralistic, entrepreneurial culture.

Electronic Frontier Foundation

815 Eddy St., San Francisco, CA 94109
(415) 436-9333
email: info@eff.org
website: www.eff.org

The Electronic Frontier Foundation was founded in July 1990 in response to a basic threat to speech. The group works with advocates worldwide to create a global digital environment that upholds both human rights and constitutional rights, and it continues to take on cutting-edge legal cases to win victories for user rights.

Electronic Privacy Information Center (EPIC)

1718 Connecticut Ave. NW, Suite 200, Washington DC 20009
(202) 483-1140
email: info@epic.org
website: www.epic.org

EPIC is a public interest research center in Washington, DC, that focuses public attention on emerging civil liberties issues and protecting privacy, freedom of expression, and constitutional values in the information age.

Federal Communications Commission (FCC)

455 Twelfth St. SW, Washington, DC 20554
(888) 225-5322
email: PRA@fcc.gov
website: www.fcc.gov

The FCC regulates interstate and international communications by radio, television, wire, satellite, and cable in all fifty states, the District of Columbia, and US territories. An independent US government agency overseen by Congress, the FCC is the federal agency responsible for implementing and enforcing America's communications law and regulations.

Federal Trade Commission (FTC)

600 Pennsylvania Ave. NW, Washington, DC 50580
(202) 326-2222
email: opa@ftc.gov
website: www.ftc.gov

The FTC pursues vigorous and effective law enforcement; advances consumers' interests by sharing its expertise with federal and state legislatures and US and international government agencies; develops policy and research tools through hearings, workshops, and conferences; and creates practical and plain-language educational programs for consumers and businesses in a global marketplace with constantly changing technologies.

Fight for the Future

PO Box 55071 #95005 Boston, MA 02205
(508) 3683026
email: team@fightforthefuture.org
website: www.fightforthefuture.org

Fight for the Future is a nonprofit organization whose mission is to ensure that the web continues to hold freedom of expression and creativity at its core. The organization envisions a world in which everyone can access the internet affordably, free of interference or censorship and with full privacy.

Foundation for Economic Education (FEE)

1819 Peachtree Rd. NE, Suite 300, Atlanta, GA 30309
(404) 554-9980
email: tucker@fee.org
website: www.fee.org

The FEE strives to bring about a world in which the economic, ethical, and legal principles of a free society are familiar and credible to the rising generation. The organization offers student seminars, free online courses, engaging classroom resources, and enlightening classic and contemporary online content.

Foundation for Individual Rights in Education (FIRE)

510 Walnut St., Suite 1250, Philadelphia, PA 19106
(215) 717-3473
email: fire@thefire.org
website: www.thefire.org

FIRE seeks to defend and sustain individual rights at America's colleges and universities. These rights include freedom of speech, legal equality, due process, religious liberty, and sanctity of conscience—the essential qualities of individual liberty and dignity.

Organization for Security and Co-operation in Europe (OSCE)

Wallnerstrasse 6, 1010 Vienna, Austria
+32 1 514 360
email: pm@osce.org
website: www.osce.org

The OSCE is a forum for political dialogue on a wide range of security issues and a platform for joint action to improve the lives of individuals and communities. The organization uses a comprehensive approach to security that encompasses the politico-military, economic and environmental, and human dimensions.

Public Knowledge

1818 N St. NW, Suite 410, Washington DC 20036
(202) 861-0020
email: pk@publicknowledge.org
website: www.publicknowledge.org

Public Knowledge promotes freedom of expression, an open internet, and access to affordable communications tools and creative works. The organization works to shape policy on behalf of the public interest.

United Nations Educational, Scientific and Cultural Organization (UNESCO)

7 place Fontenoy, 75007, Paris, France
+33 (0)1 4568 1000
website: www.unesco.org

UNESCO is responsible for coordinating international cooperation in education, science, culture, and communication. It strengthens the ties between nations and societies and mobilizes the wider public so that each child and citizen has access to quality education; may grow and live in a cultural environment rich in diversity and dialogue; can fully benefit from scientific advances; and can enjoy full freedom of expression, the basis of democracy, development, and human dignity.

Bibliography of Books

Luca Belli and Primavera De Filippi, *Net Neutrality Compendium: Human Rights, Free Competition and the Future of the Internet.* New York, NY: Springer, 2015.

Andrew Blum, *Tubes: A Journey to the Center of the Internet.* New York, NY: Ecco, 2013.

Committee on the Judiciary, United States Senate, *Why Net Neutrality Matters: Protecting Consumers and Competition Through Meaningful Open Internet Rules.* CreateSpace Independent Publishing Platform, 2017.

Susan Crawford, *Captive Audience: The Telecom Industry and Monopoly Power in the New Gilded Age.* New Haven, CT: Yale University Press, 2014.

Thomas Winslow Hazlett, *The Political Spectrum: The Tumultuous Liberation of Wireless Technology, from Herbert Hoover to the Smartphone.* New Haven, CT: Yale University Press, 2017.

Melissa Higgins and Michael Regan, *Net Neutrality* (Essential Library of the Information Age). Minneapolis, MN: Essential Library, 2016.

Matthew Howard, *Net Neutrality for Broadband: Understanding the FCC's 2015 Open Internet Order and Other Essays.* Puma Concolor Aeternus Press, 2015.

Lawrence Lessig, *Code: And Other Laws of Cyberspace, Version 2.0.* New York, NY: Basic Books, 2006.

Nate Levesque, *Please Upgrade for Access: How Your ISP Might Be Undermining Your Rights.* Independently Published, 2017.

Rebecca MacKinnon, *Consent of the Networked: The Worldwide Struggle for Internet Freedom.* New York, NY: Basic Books, 2013.

Katarina Maniadaki, *EU Competition Law, Regulation and the Internet: The Case of Net Neutrality.* New York, NY: Wolters Kluwer Law & Business, 2014.

Jeff Mapua, *Net Neutrality and What It Means to You* (Digital and Information Literacy). New York, NY: Rosen Publishing, 2017.

David E. McNabb, *Public Utilities.* 2nd ed. Northampton, MA: Edward Elgar Publishing, Inc., 2016.

Vincent Mosco, *Becoming Digital: Toward a Post-Internet Society.* Bingley, West Yorkshire, UK: Emerald Group Publishing, 2017.

Dawn C. Nunziato, *Virtual Freedom: Net Neutrality and Free Speech in the Internet Age.* Stanford, CA: Stanford Law Books, 2009.

Karl Rogers, *Media Consolidation & Net Neutrality in the U.S.* Los Angeles, CA: Trebol Press, 2017.

Florian Sprenger and Valentine A. Pakis, *The Politics of Micro-Decisions: Edward Snowden, Net Neutrality, and the Architectures of the Internet.* Saxony, Germany: Meson Press, 2015.

Zeynep Tufekci, *Twitter and Tear Gas: The Power and Fragility of Networked Protest.* New Haven, CT: Yale University Press, 2017.

Tim Wu, *The Master Switch: The Rise and Fall of Information Empires.* New York, NY: Vintage, 2011.

Bob Zelnick and Eva Zelnick, *The Illusion of Net Neutrality: Political Alarmism, Regulatory Creep and the Real Threat to Internet Freedom.* Stanford, CA: Hoover Institution Press, 2013.

Index